Praise from Influential
Thought Leaders and V
The Living Organization®

D0069864

"The Living Organization® is blazing a trail to a new world. You will never again see your organization, or relate to your employees, customers, and investors in the same old way. Norman Wolfe's insightful reframing of how business operates frees us from the shackles of the "great machine" and opens us to the possibility of realizing the fullest of our human potential, individually and collectively."

Chip Conley, Executive Chairman, Joie de Vivre and author of "Peak: How Great Companies Get Their Mojo from Maslow"

"I've always believed that people are central to the success of any organization. Norman Wolfe gets that. In his new book The Living Organization®, he guides readers through the concept of organizations as living energy. People are energy, and The Living Organization® is created by people's activities, relationships, and context regarding what they do and why they do it. This is an intriguing book."

Ken Blanchard, coauthor of The One Minute Manager® and Lead with LUV

"For successful leaders who want to get even better this book is a must read. The Living Organization® is a powerful and penetrating exploration of what really creates great companies. It completely reframes how to understand your organization while also providing a simple and pragmatic approach to achieve your loftiest dreams."

Marshall Goldsmith - million-selling author of the New York Times bestsellers, MOJO and What Got You Here Won't Get You There

"This is an inspiring reframing of how we understand business creates bottom-line result. I couldn't put it down. The Living Organization® reinforces so much of what I know to be true about the power of culture and inspiration to move organizations. Every leader will find dozens of powerful insights in this book to help engage their teams in new patterns of healthy growth and long-term success."

Casey Sheehan, CEO, Patagonia

"In today's global business world the traditional business models which rely largely on left brain quantitative thinking and actions, while still necessary are no longer sufficient. The Living organization insightfully provides many of the missing pieces. With clarity borne from years of real life experiences, Norman Wolfe reframes and broadens our understanding of how organizations can create better results. Every CEO, board member and senior executive will benefit from the practical guidance this book provides."

John Rehfeld, former GM/ CEO of Toshiba America, Seiko Instruments and Proxima corporation, currently a director of two public companies, Executive MBA professor at Pepperdine and USD, and author, Alchemy of a Leader

"Drawing on his deep and extensive experience building successful teams and organizations as a corporate manager and consultant, Norman Wolfe reveals the vibrant structure and magical process of The Living Organization® and provides a map for traversing the terrain to create an extraordinary business."

Jeff Klein, author, Working for Good: Making a Difference While Making a Living

"Have you ever wondered why some groups seem so full of energy and vitality bubbling with enthusiasm, creating results while others barely progress even with substantial prompting and pushing? In "The Living Organization" we are granted access to that hidden dynamic that controls the energy--and results--of any group. In this new insightful book, Norman Wolfe reveals a model that strengthens our ability to harness the often unconscious energetics that determine outstanding results and greatness in a company. The practical tool this book offers will allow you to enlist your group's deeper energies to drive uncommon success."

Rick Ferris, President Sequoia Realty Corp.

"We have lived for too long believing that we have to check our emotional and spiritual self at the door when we enter the world of work. No More! Norman Wolfe will expand your current thinking and reveal the very act of creating financial success requires we bring our entire self into our work. In this groundbreaking book he provides practical tools to combine the forces of our Activity, Relationship and Context to create results beyond what we thought possible."

Tom Zender, Former CEO, Unity Worldwide, Author of "God Goes to Work", Evolutionary Leader, Corporate Executive

"In today's world it is critical that businesses all across our globe act and behave from an ethical stance. In this thought provoking and insightful book, Norman Wolfe teaches that as a living being, organizations are governed by the same forces that govern all living entities. Morals and ethics no longer are an afterthought, but are shown to be at the core of creating results. This is a must read guidebook for every leader doing business in the 21st Century."

Russell Williams, CEO,
Passkeys Foundation and The Ethical Edge

"To lead today requires leveraging the power of the whole - and that requires the use of multiple intelligences. Leaders must access and draw from the living energy of organizational systems. In The Living Organization®, Norman Wolfe offers the clarity and depth of insight that comes from experience. He teaches leaders how to develop and use their cognitive, emotional and spiritual intelligences to tap the organization's intelligence. This "intelligence of the collective" is what creates extraordinary success."

Cindy Wigglesworth, President, Deep Change, Inc., Creator of the SQi
Spiritual Intelligence assessment

"The Living Organization® offers an innovative and exciting new perspective on managing organizations. This book takes the purpose of the firm from a dry afterthought to the central management issue. Managers who take its message seriously will find themselves reframing their understandings of both their organizations and their roles for the better."

Dr. Philip Bromiley, Dean's Professor of Strategic Management, Merage
School of Business, University of California, Irvine

"The world is hungry for a new paradigm of business. We can see all around us that the old ways don't work, but so many in leadership positions don't know what to do or where to turn. The Living Organization® provides a model to work with, practical steps to implement, and inspiration to keep you going. Join the movement of conscious capitalists who are making a difference in the world. This book provides you the support and guidance you need."

Judi Neal, Ph.D. Director, Tyson Center for Faith and Spirituality in the
Workplace, Author of Edgewalkers: People and Organizations that Take
Risks, Build Bridges, and Break New Ground, and co-author with Alan
Harpham of Spirituality and Project Management

THE
LIVING
ORGANIZATION

TRANSFORMING BUSINESS TO CREATE EXTRAORDINARY RESULTS

Book 1: Encounter

Sherly
It was your encouragement that
started this journey
I am forever grateful
+ A radiance of Divine
Energy

Norman Wolfe

Norman Wolfe

QUANTUM
LEADERS
PUBLISHING

The Living Organization®
Published by Quantum Leaders Publishing

ISBN: 978-0-9835310-1-2
Printed in the United States of America

This is a work of non-fiction. The ideas presented are those of the author alone. All references to possible income to be gained from the techniques discussed in this book relate to specific past examples and are not necessarily representative of any future results specific individuals may achieve.

Illustrations by Lauren Card
Cover design by Michael Glock, PhD

The Living Organization, ARC Framework, Strategic Compass, Soulful Purpose, Real Time Execution, and RTE-S are trademarks or registered trademarks of Quantum Leader, Inc.

The Living Organization is available at a discount when purchased in quantity by corporations, associations and other organizations. For information, contact Quantum Leaders Publishing at 7 Shasta, Irvine, CA 92612

The Living Organization® Trilogy

Book 1 – Encounter

Book 2 – The Journey

Book 3 – A New World

Dedication

To Gregg Gallagher

His friendship and critical thinking helped midwife this work into life.
May he bring these same qualities to his Eternal Life.

Acknowledgments

How does one begin to acknowledge all the people who have contributed to and supported my journey? There are those who have directly contributed to the writing effort, there are those who have contributed to the evolution of the models and methods presented in this book, and there are those who provided loving support and encouragement along the way.

This book, however, represents more than just the ideas, models, and methods. It is a reflection of my personal journey with creating results, both on an organizational basis and on a personal basis. My journey of development as a person is deeply entwined with the book's underlying philosophy. It is with profound gratitude that I acknowledge all the people who have contributed, consciously and unconsciously, directly and indirectly, positively and negatively, to my life, my growth and my development as a person.

I want to specifically acknowledge my three editors. Peter Gerraro was my initial writing consultant who helped get the seeds of my ideas onto paper. Through his guided interviewing he managed to convert my ideas into written form and provide the initial structure to convert a concept into a book. Paul Roberts, a master storyteller, challenged me each step of the way until I understood the story I wanted to tell. He helped me understand the fullness of the story and how it paralleled other great trilogies. Lee Pound took what was already a good story and refined it. He guided me to bring more of my life into the story, making it and the whole book more fully alive.

This book is designed to address the needs of Leadership Teams (Boards, CEOs and Executive teams) to overcome their challenges in creating desired results. Many of the theories and methods come from my work with the many clients I have been honored to serve. I want to serve them better, to make them more effective, which drives me to deepen my understanding of the dynamic forces that create or block their dreams.

This would not have been possible without the support of my many clients who allowed me to test these ideas, concepts and methods. I want to specifically acknowledge two of them.

I was first introduced to National Technical Systems in 1990 when I met one of its founders and then CEO and Chairman, Dr. Jack Lin. Jack understood the power of the unconscious forces that define success and continuously explored how best to work with these forces. This led to a culture that was open to exploring new and often non-traditional ways of creating collective results. Bill McGinnis, who replaced Jack as CEO, continued the exploration, opening himself and his executive team to work with the energies of Context and Relationship. The lessons I learned working with these two great CEOs and their teams greatly influenced what is presented in the book.

From the time Jim Summers took over as President of SafeNet Mykotronx division, he had a deep connection to the organization's Soulful Purpose™. It was this connection that has guided Jim to establish the vision of what was possible for this organization. I have had the honor of working with Jim and his team for over 8 years, taking the organization through a number of growth transitions as it doubled its size. I am deeply grateful for the opportunity to work with and learn how viewing an organization as a living entity enhances its ability to continuously improve and increases its ability to grow.

Because my life had been an exploration into improving myself to improve my personal as well as business results, it has become a tapestry of many roads exploring many disciplines. One particular path I have traveled for the past 8 years is working with my teacher, guide, and mentor Brugh Joy. I will be forever in his debt, and those who have traveled the path of Joys Jubilation with me. This journey provided me an understanding of and direct experience working with the deeper energies of what many call a Divine Mystery.

I want to also acknowledge the many consultants who have been part of Quantum Leaders since its founding in 2002 and those friends who were gracious enough to mentor and advise me on this journey. Each has left their mark on The Living Organization® and me. I specifically acknowledge three of them. Kevin McGourty was the first consultant to join Quantum Leaders and showed me that others would be willing to bring my vision to reality. Don Hicks has supported our efforts for over 5 years in defining what it takes to sell our services. This book is dedicated to Gregg Gallagher who challenged my thinking every step of the way, leading to a more robust and detailed product. Gregg passed on unexpectedly and his presence and contributions are sorely missed. Of the advisors I acknowledge Mike Kucha and David Kinnear, who brought different perspectives and helped, refine the model.

Finally I want to acknowledge two people that are closest and most dear to me. My daughter Lindsay taught me what it really means to be a parent, a custodian of another living being's spirit. She taught me how to help prepare that being to give that spirit full expression. It is this experience of guiding another being towards maturity that is the basis for how to develop an organization to fully express its spirit.

My wife Jane has taught me most of all. Not only did I learn the beauty of seeing the world through the eyes of an artist, I have also come to understand and live life as an unfolding improvisational play. She showed me the meaning and power of acceptance and gratitude. Her ability to see me as what I can be, her support through all the challenges that life can bring, and the love she openly and graciously shares, has given me the strength and confidence to pursue my dreams.

And to all of you who have chosen to read this book – Thank You!

Table of Contents

Dedication   iii

Acknowledgements   iv

Foreword   1

Introduction   4

Chapter 1 - A Shock to Our System   11
A New Paradigm for Capitalism   14
The Forces of Creation   16
Evolve or Die   19

Chapter 2 - The Living Organization® - The Secret of Life   21
More than the Physical   23
The Magic of Living Organizations   24
More than a call for Social Good   25
Wisdom of manifestation   29

Chapter 3 - It's all about Energy   31
Results are energies transformed   32
Forms of Energy   32
The patterns of our lives   34
People Are Energy Too   35
Choice lets energy flow   36
The Dance of energy   38
Energy patterns that create are alive   39
The Evolutionary Flow of Energy   41

Chapter 4 - The Energy of Business   45
The Flow   46
The Source of All Energy: Our People   50

Chapter 5 - Profit: The Good, Bad and Ugly   54
The Need for Feedback   54
The Nature of Profit   56

Chapter 6 - The Rainbow Within   63
Activity - the Energy of Doing   64
Relationship - the Energy of Interactions   65

Chapter 7 - Synergy - The Multiplier Effect   68
Synergy Explained   71

Chapter 8 - Experience: The Driver of Perceived Value   76
Perception produces margin   79

Chapter 9 - Where the Magic Hides   81
Context - the Energy of Meaning and Purpose   81
The Soul of the Organization   84
Access the Wisdom   87
What gets measured gets improved   91
Explaining the Unexplainable   92
All Results Start In the Context Field   93
The Dance of Energy   94
It's All a Story   96

Chapter 10 - The True Nature of Business   100
Business in 3-D   100
A Success Story   103
The Model Applied   103
Activity   105
Relationship   106
Context   107

Chapter 11 - Putting it all Together   110
A New field – Strategy Execution   111
Strategy Execution 3.0   112
Strategic Planning is Dead – Long Live Strategy Execution   117
Start with a Compass!   120
Soulful Purpose™   121
The Mission   122
Future Vision   123
Core Values   124
Alignment is the key   125
The title, the lyrics and the music   128

Chapter 12 - Executing in Real Time   130
Real Time Execution System™ (RTE-S™)   130
It's about time   131
Alignment   133

Know your Place   135
What to do, what to do?   135
Get ready the future is coming   138
Incrementing or Innovating – It makes a difference   139
Who's changing what   141
What's your horizon?   142
Put your money where your mouth is   144
Who dreamed this up anyway?   145
What did you assume?   146
Lights, Cameras, Action   146
Well, how did you do?   147
Who's leading the show?   150
Speaking of Boards   152
The Journey of Development   153

Chapter 13 - The Journey Continues   155

Appendix   159
Business as the Driving Force of Society   159
How Capitalism's Reputation Changed   160
The Evolution of Business   162
The Limitations of Worldviews   162
The Organization as Machine   163
The Impact of World War II   165
Our Changing Worldview   166
The Emergence of the Humanistic View   168
Humanism Isn't Enough   174
The Leadership Challenge   179

Book References   181

Endnotes   187

Index   190

About the Author   195

Foreword

By John Mackey, Co-CEO, Whole Foods Market

Do we need a new way to think about business, corporations, and capitalism for the 21st Century? Do we need to create a new business paradigm? Corporations are probably the most influential institutions in the world today and yet many people do not believe that they can be trusted. Instead corporations are widely perceived as greedy, selfish, exploitative, uncaring – and interested only in maximizing profits. In the early years of the 21st century, major ethical lapses on the part of big business contributed to a growing distrust of business. Increasingly, many people believe there must be something wrong with both corporations and capitalism.

The problem does not lie in the system of capitalism but rather in the theories we use to guide our decisions. Although economic theory has evolved since Adam Smith wrote *The Wealth of Nations* in 1776, many economists continue using industrial and machine metaphors to explain how the economy works. According to this model, business operates like a machine—business owners input various amounts of capital, labor, and land at the start. Profits then spit out on the other side of the metaphorical machine.

Today's real challenge for the corporation and the economy overall, is that most modern economists and business leaders' thinking is still grounded in a theoretical model that does not acknowledge the complex interdependencies of all the various constituencies and all the dynamics that impact success. The existing model simply fails to provide sufficient guidance for success in the 21st Century.

For business to reach its fullest potential in the 21st Century, we need a new business paradigm that moves beyond simplistic machine/industrial models to one that embraces the complexity and interdependencies, in which corporations exist today. Complexity and interdependency is our reality and our economic and business theories need to evolve to reflect this truth.

The Living Organization® is that evolutionary perspective. It presents a fresh new way to understand what an organization is and how it operates. It directs us to understand how organizations draw from complexity and interdependence to develop, grow and evolve. We begin to see businesses as living entities in relationship with all its stakeholders, which is all part of an evolutionary journey for advancing society. This is the same fascinating discovery I made over the last 30 years as CEO of Whole Foods Market.

When Whole Foods Market's co-founders created the company in 1980 we infused it with a few simple ideals and core values and then created very simple business structures to help fulfill those ideals. However, as the company grew a process of dynamic self-organization took place to fulfill the original purpose. The business and even the purpose evolved over time through the dynamic interaction of the various interdependent stakeholders with each other and with the business itself. This interactive relationship of an organization with all its stakeholders (customers, employees, investors, suppliers, and the community) is what is so richly expressed in The Living Organization®. It provides a deeper understanding into why Whole Foods Market consistently created success for all the stakeholders and why our purpose has become deeper, richer, and more complex over the years.

Through the lens of The Living Organization®, we can see the solutions to many of our challenges as a business and within society. A business as a machine does not, and cannot, have any social consciousness or social responsibility. A business viewed as a living entity is, like all people within a society, a citizen with a social and moral responsibility to both itself and society. A machine does not learn and adapt to its environment, but adaptation is the very essence of all living entities. Machines merely produce, they cannot innovate, while living entities can actually dream of and create a healthier future.

Every successful CEO and organization leader will find within the pages of The Living Organization® the same secrets of success they have learned over the course of their careers, only it will look very different. It does not read like a traditional business book providing a rehashing of the same old management theories. It does not reject the traditional theories; rather it adds to and expands them. It provides a fresh new perspective that can deepen our understanding of the things that successful CEOs have stumbled on through trial and error.

Because it is a new paradigm that draws from many disciplines, it will challenge us. It will challenge the way we think, it will challenge how we interact with our employees, our suppliers, our customers, our investors and our communities. It will challenge us to grow up, become more conscious and like all living entities, evolve.

When we are small children we are egocentric, concerned only about our own needs and desires. As we mature, we expand our consciousness and grow beyond this egocentrism; we begin to care about others – our families, friends, communities, and countries. Our capacity to love can expand even further, to loving people from different races, religions, and countries – potentially to unlimited love for all people and even for other sentient creatures. This is the potential of human beings, expanding consciousness and taking joy in the flourishing of people and other living beings everywhere.

Living Organizations® also have the potential to evolve in consciousness, and the collection of all businesses can evolve towards a conscious capitalism. Let each organization leader, whether for-profit, non-profit or government, learn the art of leading a Living Organization®; of guiding its growth and development towards greater consciousness to better serve its customers and in turn further the advancement of a healthy society.

Introduction

As a professional magician I am sworn, on the graves of Houdini, Blackstone, and all the other great magicians, to never reveal the secrets behind the magic. Today I am about to break that vow. I am going to reveal the secret behind the magic. Not the magic behind creating the illusion we see on the stage, but the magic behind creating the results we get in business and in life.

Every CEO Executive, team leader and even every individual contributor wants to create the results they set as their goals. This is certainly true for me. This desire led me on a continual journey of exploration and discovery to answer the questions, "How are results created, what is the trick to improving my success rate, and why does the same effort sometimes produce results and sometimes not?"

This journey has two parallel paths, my business career and my personal growth and development. These two paths are not separate and distinct paths but are an interwoven journey of reaching and seeking, attempts and failures, and the eventual success that follows. Mostly it is a journey of discovery, a journey that has revealed to me much about the secrets that lie behind the results we create, of how and why we get the results we get.

Two days stand out in my mind, two days that marked the beginning of two distinct journeys. Two journeys that would over time merge into a single journey.

March 4, 1969 was a beautiful sunny day in New York, the first day of spring-like weather after a long cold winter. I was a senior at NYU and a group of us spent the day in Bear Mountain State Park enjoying the coming of spring. It was also the beginning of Purim; the Jewish holiday that celebrates the end of the dark of winter and the coming light of spring.

I had spent the evening with a group of Jewish students who were celebrating with music and songs that brought me back to my youth and family gatherings.

When I returned to my room, I felt the sweetness of the day mixed with longing for days past, the interplay of joy and sadness. My roommate was there and as we talked he pulled out a book by Alan Watts. He read a passage, "To know white you must know black, to know up, down must exist." In a flash I was transformed.

I didn't know what an epiphany meant until years later but in that moment I experienced what would certainly be an epiphany: a spontaneous understanding, what some might call a spontaneous awakening. In that moment my world flashed in front of me. People formed a circle before my eyes and as each person's face appeared a sense of deep understanding and pure love filled me.

This deep loving feeling stayed with me for months and it seemed my relationship with everything in life was vivid, peaceful and loving. I began reading Alan Watts, Herman Hesse, Joseph Campbell and others. My whole world began to re-form and I was filled with a purpose to journey into a deeper understanding of life, a journey of spiritual discovery that to this day is a significant part of my life.

I took this newfound awareness with me upon graduation as I entered the world of work. I started my career as a system analyst for Pratt & Whitney Aircraft designing applications and writing code for fuel cell testing. It was a very different world from the open exploration into the deeper mysteries that dominated my previous six months.

Where the one tapped into the mystical, curious, discovery side of me, the world of computers engaged the logical, analytical rational parts of my being. I found that the two worlds, while very distinct, seemed to draw on each other. My analytical side made sense of the mystical discoveries I would have and the mystical creative side brought innovative approaches to the challenges of logic and program design.

I entered on the second path of my journey on July 19, 1976. I remember this day so vividly because like my day of awakening, the events of that day marked what might be called a second awakening, but of a different kind.

My wife and I just returned from two weeks visiting the UK during the bi-centennial anniversary of the United States. We were visiting the very place from which our country was born, born not out of intention but out of conflict. We were visiting the culture that rejected our forefathers and now embraced us as friends.

I was returning to work this day, renewed, rejuvenated and filled with a new sense of beginning. I was just completing my first year as manager of a Service District for Hewlett Packard. It was not an easy year for me, struggling with the role of management and the challenges it brought forth. I knew I had a lot to learn, but was eager to jump in and conquer this like I did everything else in my life.

The first person I saw was my boss, who called me into his office to give me my performance review. As I sat and read his comments and his ranking I was devastated. It seems in his opinion I did not do one thing right. The ratings were unacceptable in every category. I was a complete and utter failure.

How could this be? I knew I had some struggles, I knew I had a lot to learn, but completely unacceptable?

I began questioning whether I was really cut out for management. My whole career I had always received outstanding reviews. It was the innovative work I did at Pratt & Whitney using HP's computers that landed me the job as Systems Engineer for HP in Southern California. The outstanding work I was doing as System Engineer, with both the sales people and customers, caused my current boss to offer me the position of District Service Manager.

I was excited when I was given the opportunity to move into management for I was convinced I could really help the people who worked for me to be as successful in their careers as I was. Still filled with the earlier discoveries of how life worked, of love and caring for others, I knew I could help others become successful.

But now after this review I wasn't sure. Perhaps I should return to the world of computers where I was safe and successful. Computers, after all, were logical, results definable and predictable. Not so with people. And though I was very successful in dealing with customers there seemed to be something more when it came to leading an organization.

But a number of other managers, my peers and superiors, individuals who would become mentors and coaches, saw something in me I did not yet see. They encouraged me to stick with management believing I had all the attributes to become a great leader. It was good they believed in me for at that time I had great doubts. But I chose to heed their advice and I am really glad I did.

For this started my second journey, the one of discovering what it took to successfully lead an organization. Out of conflict was born a new determination, a determination to discover the secrets of business and organization success.

And so I set out to become an expert at managing organizations and the people who comprised them. And like every manager, I hungered for one thing – to always achieve the goals I set for my organization. Many of these goals were mine, a sense of purpose I wanted my organizations to achieve, which of course were merged with goals given me by my boss, or later when I was COO or CEO, the ones established by the boards of directors or investors. Regardless of who established the goals, all that mattered to me was exceeding them.

I have spent the last 40 years of my life traveling these two paths. The first is a spiritual path delving ever deeper into the mysteries of why I do what I do, how do I create what I want and why life unfolds the way it does. The second path is that of achieving business results, growth, profits, and improved performance. These two paths continually intersect, cross over, circle around and intermingle with each other. There always seemed to be parallels I could draw on from one path that provided insights into the challenges of the other.

It wasn't until the early part of this century, as I was working on defining the purpose and mission of Quantum Leaders that I began to get a sense that what for many years seemed to me to be two very different paths were in fact the same path. They were both complementary sides of the same coin, the same journey; a journey to find the secret formula for success in all endeavors of life – a philosopher's stone that will guarantee the success of any organization and the people within it.

This journey led to the development of The Living Organization® model – the subject of this book.

I have written this book because I sense there is a major change happening in the ranks of corporate leadership, a generational shift in the ranks of CEOs and other corporate level executives. It is a shift from those who were raised during World War II and moved into leadership roles during the 70s and 80s, to those who were raised in the post Vietnam era and came into the leadership roles in the 90s and turn of the century.

The previous generation relied on military, hierarchical organization, command and control leadership. The new generation was schooled in the power of teams, global collaboration and empowerment of employees. But the old paradigm still has a hold on the system and prevents these ideas from taking hold.

This generational shift in leadership coincides with the recognition that what worked in the past is not working any more. "What got us here won't get us there," the title of Marshal Goldsmith's latest book declares. There is a breakdown of our existing business models and the new leaders sense it. If the recent economic crisis has taught us anything, it is that the future will not look like the past. The framework, the very paradigm we have used to guide our efforts in creating results no longer produces the same level of results. Some even question whether it works at all. The magic has left us, or so it seems. In reality the magic is still there. It is simply that we never understood the whole picture of how we did what we did. We simply lack the insight, the details of how the magic of creating results actually works.

This book is for those new leaders who are seeking to better understand how to navigate the multiplicity of dynamics impacting their organizations. It presents the foundation of a new business model, keeping what is valid from its predecessor models, adding new concepts to create a consolidated framework that brings it all together. This book provides today's leaders a new, more detailed map to navigate the complex business world of this century.

We start by explaining the need for a new business model, revealing the limitations of the existing paradigm, while also recognizing what elements are still important going forward. We then lay the foundation of the new paradigm, The Living Organization® model. By shifting the lens from the organization as a machine of production to a living creator of results we can begin to get a glimpse of how this will reveal many heretofore secrets of success, Chapters 1 & 2.

Key to every living entity, key to life itself is the understanding that everything is energy. In Chapter 3 we present an overview of the nature of energy and its role in creating results. With this understanding we will take you through the process of how energy flows through an organization on its journey of transformation into creating the desired results. It describes the role each of the domains of business – people, process, customers and financial – plays in the transformation process. We show where the old paradigm fits in the new model, keeping what is valid from the former approaches while adding new concepts to create a more robust holistic organic framework for today's leaders, Chapters 4 - 10.

While having a model that is robust enough to describe the forces impacting success in today's fast shifting environment, it is not sufficient. In Chapters 11 & 12 we delineate a management process that allows the organization leaders, the CEO and executive team, a department head, a team leader or even an individual, to manage the execution, the process of activity needed to achieve the results. This new approach, The Real Time Execution System™, builds on many of the tools and processes that have been developed over the last 3 – 4 decades to improve an organization's success in achieving its goals. But The Real Time Execution System™ is not constrained by trying to fit itself into a machine, a paradigm that inherently limits the release of the creative forces needed for successful execution. Instead it is rooted in The Living Organization® model providing access and the ability to work with the very forces that breed creativity, passion, engagement, commitment, synergy, unparalleled customer experience and all the other drivers of success.

You are likely to find many of the concepts presented familiar though not necessarily through the lens of business. I draw on many fields of study including physics, psychology, perennial wisdoms, philosophy, and of course business. In some cases I have left untouched the work of others, merely merging it in where I believe it fits best. In other cases I have taken previous work and modified it, either adding concepts or simply reframing them. I have also drawn on work not normally associated with business, recognizing the business is also part of the totality of life.

Like all new discoveries we have the distinct advantage of having available to us the many contributions that have come before. I have built on the work of others and my own "eureka moments," assembling the puzzle pieces to form a more complete picture of how modern corporations function, and how their resources can better be harnessed to achieve the goals of management and the communities they serve – their "marketplace of customers." This model is part of an emerging paradigm – the next rung on the evolutionary ladder of organizational theory.

Like all journeys, we are served by having an effective map to guide us. In many regards I felt like an explorer on a journey wandering though many uncharted regions. It is my hope that this book will serve as an effective map guiding the next generation of leaders as they navigate the challenges of our current and ever changing business environment.

> *"The dogmas of the quiet past are inadequate to the stormy present. The occasion is piled high with difficulty, and we must rise with the occasion. As our case is new, so we must think anew and act anew."* **Abraham Lincoln**

A Shock to Our System

It's April 3, 2010. At Apple Stores all across the United States, hundreds of people are lined up eager to grab their very own iPad, finally available after two months of unending promotion. When the doors finally opened, people piled in to be one of the first to own an iPad. Within the first month Apple sold over a million iPads and by March 2011 was up to over 15 million units and climbing.

This was more than just another successful launch of a new Apple product. It was another record breaking launch in a string that started with the iPhone in June 2007, the iPhone 3G in 2008, and the iPhone 3GS in 2009. Each launch drew thousands of buyers waiting in lines at Apple stores and sold millions of products, including 33.75 million iPhones.

Apple achieved the highest volume of sales for any product launch and they did it in the middle of the worst recession since the 1930s; in a market where companies like Bear Stearns and Lehman Brothers were collapsing, banks needed huge bailouts to stay in business, and the once great General Motors ("what's good for GM is good for the United States") became the property of the United States government.

Every executive, every leader, no matter the size of their organization or their position within it, has the same overriding objective - to create their desired results. And what leader does not set out to go beyond just creating average results? Every leader has visions of leading their organizations to stand out from the pack, to manifest results that would be considered magical, results like those Steve Jobs, and his team at Apple, consistently repeats with each new product launch.

"Apple sold 15 million iPads in nine months, created a mammoth new product category and started an industry of copycats. Apparently, it doesn't pay to bet against Jobs' gut instinct[1]."

Is Apple's repeated success a fluke that is unique to them, is it Steve Jobs' unique "gut instinct" that creates Apple's magic, or is there a set of principles that can truly explain Apple's success?

This book will explain what truly underlies Apple's success by looking at the world of creating results from a completely different vantage point. It will provide insights and practices that will allow any company to achieve the magical results of Apple and others. Yes, Apple is not alone in consistently creating results that go beyond great; there are many other companies who have demonstrated similar success during these difficult times that follow a similar pattern.

In his book *Firms of Endearment*, Raj Sisodia has identified a number of companies who march to a different drummer. These Firms of Endearment (FoE) companies not only embrace the traditional business paradigm, they add to it a set of principles that transcend merely improving the effectiveness of the machine of production. Like all companies, they pay attention to increasing efficiency, cutting costs and maximizing shareholder value, but go beyond these traditional objectives. They add a sense of higher purpose, of caring for and being in service to employees, customers, partners, investors, and the greater society.

Who are these companies and what results do they produce? We all know them and most people aspire to be like them in one form or another. The 30 companies Sisodia studied, all highly admired and often loved by their customers, are Amazon, BMW, CarMax, Caterpillar, Commerce Bank, The Container Store, Costco, eBay, Google, Harley-Davidson, Honda, IDEO, IKEA, JetBlue, Johnson & Johnson, Jordan's Furniture, L.L.Bean, New Balance, Patagonia, REI, Southwest, Starbucks, Timberland, Toyota, Trader Joe's, UPS, Wegmans, and Whole Foods.

As for results, over the ten years ending June 30, 2006 they produced a return on investment of 1,026% compared to the S&P's return of 128%.

And during the last five years they have produced a return of 240% compared with the S&P's return of -13%.

Apple is no fluke, nor is the performance of the FoE companies. These companies perform well and often have a loyal following usually reserved for rock stars and sports teams for a reason. These companies don't simply produce results, they consistently create magic.

But is it magic? I want to tell you something about magic. At one point in my life I was a professional magician, performing every week for three months at a local nightclub. For everyone in the audience, what I did amazed them, wowed them and stupefied them. They couldn't figure out how the coins could possibly disappear and reappear right in front of their eyes. To them it was simply magic. To me, however, it was not magic. I knew the secrets that lie below the surface. I knew how to create the illusion.

Arthur C. Clark said, "Any sufficiently advanced technology is indistinguishable from magic."[2] I believe the corollary is also true. What appears to be magic is in reality an advanced technology that is not yet fully understood.

The magical results of Apple, the FoE companies and others only appear to be magic. In reality it is the combination of certain forces, certain energies that logically and rationally produce their results. It appears to be magic because we do not have a good model that explains these forces and how to work with them.

What we need is a new model for business that more fully explains the forces that underlie the creation of magical results, a new model that explains how to manifest the same magical results created by Apple, the FoE companies and many other companies that consistently perform at these levels even if they do not make it to the public limelight.

This book will provide such a model, an evolutionary model that builds on our current models for business success and expands them to explain what they miss or ignore. It will provide a deep understanding of how to work with the forces that mix together to produce the results we create. It will provide the map that will allow you to lead your organization to create the desired outcomes, which to others will appear magical.

But it will not be easy. While the principles may be easy to understand, they will not be easy to adopt and implement. It will call on you to rethink how you believe results are created. You may find yourself standing alone against other advisors, your staff, even your board and your investors.

Our world is undergoing tectonic changes, major shifts in the rules of engagement, the way things get done. No matter where we look, politics, education, the environment, and business are in turmoil. Nothing is stable any more. The maps we've used to navigate our world no longer give us the proper guidance they once did.

When our world seems turned upside down, when everything seems uncertain and unpredictable, the natural response is to return to the comfort of what used to work. There is a natural tendency to call for a reinvigoration of what we used to do, to fall back on the old rules of engagement, even in the face of mounting data that the old ways don't work. Everywhere you turn people will be suggesting a return to fundamentals, to the rules of the "good old days." This is why it will be challenging to move to a new way of thinking and why it will take courage to adopt a new model for business success.

But as difficult as it will be, do we have a choice? Can we continue to rely on what has worked in the past but is now failing? To paraphrase Einstein's famous observation, "The significant problems we have cannot be solved by the same type of thinking that created them." Or as a dear friend and client, Bill McGinnis, CEO of National Technical Systems, is fond of quoting Mark Twain, "If you always do what you have always done, then you will always get the same results you have always gotten."

I believe that it is at these very times, when the old rules of engagement are failing and our world feels in chaos, that we need the courage to explore and be open to taking steps we have never taken before. This is the very time when we should consider what we rejected in the past. That is what creating magic is about: doing what others do not expect is possible.

A New Paradigm for Capitalism

The world of commerce has evolved over hundreds of years. Society has evolved from a purely agrarian society to an industrial society. Our world has been on a journey that has taken us from a society of hunters and farmers to craftsman to the modern corporation of efficient production. The rules of commerce have evolved during this journey to the system we call capitalism and the capitalist system has been the engine of progress in every society that has adopted it.

Progress, innovation, and improving the standard of living is what business used to be all about from the early days of mercantilism through the industrial revolution; that is until business turned from being the engine of creation, the source of progress, to the machine of destruction[3].

Can this system, which created widespread success for over 300 years, function in today's society? Can we still depend on the model that advanced society for so many centuries? Is the very foundation upon which our society is built, free market capitalism, failing us as a system?

At first glance, it might seem that the evidence is heavily weighted towards yes. What we hear in the press and the problems I have mentioned earlier indicate that capitalism has had its day and that we need a new system.

Let's remember the incredible progress capitalism and the individual businesses that follow its principles have collectively created over the last three centuries and resist the temptation to throw out the baby with the bath water. Much is right with our system. We must resist the impulse to discredit and discard our economic model just because it doesn't seem to work right now. It could well be the system of economic exchange is sound but its application has been limited.

Yes, Lehman Brothers and Bear Sterns are gone from the scene and the Federal Government owns GM. Yes, housing values have plummeted and many people have lost a significant amount of their net worth. Yes, unemployment is currently at a painful 9% - 10%. Yet many companies survive and even thrive.

Think again about Apple's extremely successful launches of the iPhone and the iPad. As Sarah Rotman Epps of Forrester Research said, "The iPad isn't behaving like other consumer devices. It has a steamroller of momentum behind it that indicates incredibly strong demand for this entirely new form factor."[4]

If Apple, FoE companies and the companies I work with as a consultant can create such magic, why not all companies? Why not your company?

The system has its flaws but all human systems have their flaws. I contend that the basic principles of Capitalism are sound. Rather than declare it a failure, let's see if we can discover how to enhance its positive attributes while eliminating the negative impacts. Can we create a system that draws on the productive, society-benefiting aspects of capitalism while eliminating its negative side effects? Can the decisions made by our corporate leaders to create their desired results and benefit their organizations, also benefit society? My journey to discover an answer to how results are created also revealed the answer to these questions, which will be revealed in this book and the works that will follow.

I have discovered that the flaw is not the inherent nature of the system but our limited understanding of its inner workings. The framework by which we make decisions within the system is what is causing the system to fail. Put another way, there is nothing wrong with the territory that we are traveling over; our maps simply do not show the full range of terrain. Is it any wonder that every now and then we fall into a pit of quicksand or get caught in a raging river? What is missing from our understanding? What does our current map, our current business model, not reveal?

The Forces of Creation

Given my background as an engineer, I first looked at business from a scientific perspective, seeing it as a system of dynamic forces. I used Force Field analysis to help me explain, identify, and organize the forces that create society's situation. Force Field analysis (FFA) is a simple tool developed by Kurt Lewin, the founder of social psychology and one of the first to study group dynamics and organizational development. FFA changed social science and is regularly used for strategic planning.[5]

In Figure 1 I show how this technique provides a framework for looking at the factors (forces) that influence any situation. It asks what forces drive movement towards a goal (driving forces) or block movement from reaching a goal (restraining forces). A similar pairing of forces drives our Capitalist system as a whole, as well as each company within it.

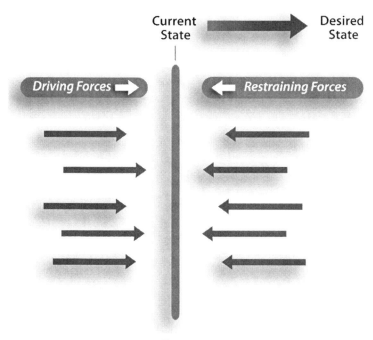

Figure 1

The challenge in analyzing any system is to identify all of the critical forces operating in it. Yet, it is difficult to identify all the forces because of the limiting nature of our worldview. Our individual and collective worldview serves to frame how we understand our world and it also has the characteristic of limiting the information available to us.

When we thought the world was flat, we could not imagine sailing to an undiscovered continent. We couldn't even imagine such land masses existed. When we believed the earth was the center of the universe, we had no way to truly understand the motion of the planets. Our current worldview about how we create results will be our challenge. It will challenge our ability to look beyond our worldview so we can understand all the forces operating within an economic system of exchange.

Every new discovery challenges some aspect of the old paradigm. The first response from orthodoxy is to reject the new discovery or try to explain it within the existing framework. When the evidence becomes so strong that it exposes the inability of the existing paradigm to fully explain how the world works, a new paradigm evolves. Until then, the forces not fully explained by the current paradigm are relegated to the mystical or the magical.

For example, James Clerk Maxwell developed an accurate theory of electromagnetism by showing that light was electromagnetic radiation operating in the same field that enabled electrical and magnetic phenomena, a field he called the ether. While this advanced the field of classical physics and explained phenomena that could not otherwise be explained, it never explained the forces that lie in this field or how they impacted the world. The ether remained a mystery until the advent of Quantum Physics began to peer under the veil of the subatomic world.

Likewise, forces operating on our economic system today are still relegated to the ether for the same reason. For example, in his attempt to explain the self-regulating nature of the marketplace, Adam Smith wrote, "...and by directing his effort in such a manner as to produce the greatest value for his own gain, he is in this, as in many other cases, led by an **invisible hand** (emphasis added) to promote an end which was no part of his intention."[6]

Like the ether of Maxwell's classical physics, Smith could only recognize that there were impactful forces at play but couldn't fully explain them. To this day, most economists still accept there are forces which we don't fully understand or see that regulate the market.

A *New York Times* headline on September 2, 2010 reads, **"Bernanke Says He Failed To See Financial Flaws."** In the article Mr. Bernanke, the Chairman of the Federal Reserve Bank, says, *"What I did not recognize was the extent to which the system had flaws and weaknesses in it that were going to amplify the initial shock from sub-prime and make it into a much bigger crisis."*

The forces acting on a system are present whether we recognize them or not. As described by FFA some of the forces drive success while others restrain success. And as Bernanke and others learned, some of the forces are visible and known while others that are not visible can have a tremendous impact.

Take the performance of two teams for example both performing the same activities. One team is highly aligned while the other is fairly dysfunctional. The aligned team will enhance its chances of success while the dysfunctional team may still perform but the path to success will be more difficult. The invisible force of alignment plays a critical role in determining which team will outperform the other. Yet, because it is in the "ether," alignment is not usually a force most managers actively take into account or even know how to work with. Similarly the unconsciously formed culture of an organization can be a force that energizes the group or it could be a force that prevents the group from changing.

Some forces carry with them shadow forces. Microsoft's success led it to take on an air of arrogance, a force that is often lying in the shadow of success. This arrogance led to many of its troubles with regulatory agencies around the globe. Because our maps are so limited, the forces that lurk in the shadows will often have unpredictable side effects.

Shadowy forces aren't inherently bad. They are merely another set of forces that affect our success. The problem arises when our maps do not help us understand their existence. Once understood they can be the source of our greatest development. Psychologist Carl Jung pointed out that when a person learns to integrate their shadow side, the result is greater maturity and wisdom. The same is true for business and our capitalist system. Fire can warm us or burn us. Business can advance society or destroy it. Only through a deeper understanding of the elemental forces can we, as Jung said, reach wisdom.

The only proper response to today's crises is to understand all the forces impacting the results we create, the visible and the invisible, the light and the shadow. Effective managers will find a new way to understand and use all these forces to create magic. When we understand how to work them, we will make the next quantum leap in improving ourselves, our companies, and our society.

The successes of Apple, Whole Foods, Container Store and the many other companies thriving during these troubled times provide powerful lessons for us. In true scientific fashion, we will reveal and explore the forces, both driving and restraining, that explain the results we observe.

We will make visible the forces that remain hidden because of the limitations of our existing paradigm. Only then can we understand and unleash the hidden magic that lies within all of our organizations.

Evolve or Die

When a system goes into chaos as capitalism is doing today, when all the old rules no longer apply, we can experience it as a failure of the system. Viewed another way, however, it becomes the natural pattern of evolution.

Evolution, a force of nature that is at times dormant, asserts itself when a species or a system no longer fits its current environment. It asserts itself by creating a crisis that forces the system to adapt to the new environment or die. A similar call to adapt and change has brought us to a critical point in our evolutionary development. The choices we make now will determine the future of business and society.

CHAPTER 2

> *"Life has its own hidden forces, which you can*
> *only discover by living."*
> **Soren Kierkegaard**

The Living Organization® - The Secret of Life

To understand what underlies the performance of all magical organizations, we need to remove the mental filters that prevent us from having a more robust understanding of the world around us. Just as we needed to build new devices to view the hidden elements that Einstein's theories predicted, we need to create a new mental lens to view the unseen forces in today's new world of business and how they manifest their magical results.

My journey to understanding how results are actually created started with my first management position at Hewlett Packard back in 1975 (where I spent the next 13 years rapidly moving up the ladder dealing with ever increasing levels of complexity). I left HP in 1988 and have spent the last 23 years working with a vast array of companies in a variety of industries. Through these years, I continued to focus on one question above all others: How do we manifest the results we desire? I dove deeper and deeper to understand why some companies possess that "magic touch" while others don't.

As the head of numerous enterprises and organizations, I soon developed the skills needed to build a smooth running and highly effective machine. I could plan, organize and control with the best of them. But with the development of each new organizational skill, something seemed to be missing. While the science of management was easy to learn, the art of leadership was much more difficult and elusive. Yet I knew I would find most of the secrets I sought in this often-discussed but not well-understood field.

In addition to developing my business skills, the desire to delve deeper into the art of creating magical results led me to explore anything that would illuminate manifestation. This journey took me into diverse religions and deep spiritual practices along with the more practical fields of physics, psychology and microbiology. I even explored mythology and mystic practices to see if I couldn't unlock the great mystery of magical transformation.

Along the way, I discovered a common thread of wisdom that flowed through this eclectic group of disciplines that better explained how we, as living beings, survive, thrive and create results in our lives. I also recognized the uncanny connection between living organizations and living organisms and how that metaphor could open up new dimensions in leadership and organizational thinking.

The Living Organization® model synthesizes what I have learned. It reveals the secrets I discovered that show how your organization can respond to the changing dynamics of today's environment and create magic in the process.

When a corporation organizes, it is "incorporated." That word derives from Latin roots and literally means, "to create a body." I believe that organizations are bodies in more than metaphorical terms and they are more than just physical bodies; they are bodies that house living beings in every sense of the word. Even American and British court systems treat them as "persons" with the same rights as any individual.

Like all forms of life, organizations create by taking in energy and transforming it into something else. In plants, it's called photosynthesis. With corporations, it's called production. Both allow the organism to serve something greater than itself.

Like people, plants and other living organisms, corporations are born, grow old, and die. They are governed by the same laws of life as other living beings and follow the same hierarchy of need fulfillment as people do. They are an intrinsic part of life, particularly in our post-modern society. They marry through mergers and give rise to offspring (or spin-offs). When they mature, they have the choice of rebirthing, of branching off in new directions (new markets, new products or totally new business models), or withering away and dying (when they are sold off or go out of business).

Each life cycle event leads The Living Organization® to the possibility of a new, more expanded way of life. This more developed stage hopefully contributes to the society around it and the living cells, the people, which give life to it. Like all living beings, corporations will either adapt to a changing environment or be driven to extinction. Yet even in dying, they can open the way for new companies to prosper and grow as they provide the seeds for new organizations to sprout to life.

The Living Organization® model views the organization as a complex, adaptable, living being. It is modeled after the greatest organization alive, an organization that manages trillions of workers as they perform their individual and collective functions in one of the most complex yet highly efficient and effective collaborative efforts ever imagined: the magnificent and magical human body.

More than the Physical

Every living body is affected by physical laws, by the laws of pressure, volume and temperature. Our blood flows according to the laws of fluid mechanics and our mental activity is measured by electro-magnetic currents. But just because our bodily functions can be explained by the laws of physics, does that make us a well-oiled machine?

Like human beings, organizations are governed by the same laws of physics that define how mechanical machines operate. Therefore elements of the traditional machine paradigm are still necessary and valuable, and we must continue to embrace them. While necessary, the model of the organization as a machine to be optimized is not sufficient. Like the human body, our organizations are more than well-oiled machines.

Forces that transcend the explanations offered by the laws of physics alone govern our human lives. Even our venerated western medical profession is slowly accepting the idea that some forces that affect human health and life are beyond present scientific understanding. For example, we don't fully appreciate the mind-body connection but accept it as fact. We would love to capture and bottle the unexplainable intuitive insight that turns out to be right, and the amazing power of "synergy." We'd love to emulate and master the "sixth sense" or "magic touch" that we often see as keys to success.

There are powerful forces in our universe (and the world of business). Many people will not try to explain or even understand these phenomena. Some will simply accept that results happen and believe we are not meant to know why they occur. Some will view them as miracles or blessings if they are good or punishment for sin if they are bad. Others will view them simply as magic (white magic for the good stuff and black magic for the bad stuff). And who doesn't love to believe in magic?

The Magic of Living Organizations

Most businesses that create magical results can't explain how they do it. Steve Jobs and his team at Apple regularly seem to pull rabbits out of their hats, but can they teach others how the trick is done? Academics and consultants study these companies and attempt to explain how they achieve "greatness." Popular books like *Good to Great* by Jim Collins help us study and define what made them great. Yet not all have remained great, as we witness one giant after another, from GM to IBM, fall from grace. Even my alma mater, the once venerated Hewlett Packard, the icon of Silicon Valley, has been plagued with scandal and a loss of its soul.

Clearly, there is something not yet explained at work that impacts the results we experience, an intricate dance between the physical world and the unseen universe. Like physics revealing the workings of Maxwell's "ether," we can begin to reveal the invisible workings of the "invisible hand" that Adam Smith first identified in the 1700's[7]. It is no longer necessary to simply think of it as unknowable invisible forces, or define it as the power of the "hand of God" or even simply magic at play.

To do so we must recognize that what limits our ability to see these forces and clouds our vision is the very thing that helps us succeed in life, our current worldview. As discussed earlier, our worldviews organize our world and at the same time limit our world. We need a new paradigm that helps us understand and see these hidden forces so we can use them in our daily decisions. We need a new, stronger, sharper lens to bring them into focus, a lens that will allow us to zoom out and see more of the world around us. Just as physics needs to transcend the mechanistic view of classical Newtonian physics, we need to replace the rational, mechanistic paradigm that currently blinds us to the all the forces impacting our results and limiting our range of choices.

The real reason we can't copy the success of the *Good to Great* companies or understand their eventual decline is because we continue to view the workings of the modern corporation through the lens of the old machine paradigm. This lens is simply not wide enough or powerful enough to reveal the forces that create success and failure in today's world.

More than a call for Social Good

This book is not the first to call for fundamental change in our foundational paradigm. The Corporate Social Responsibility (CSR) movement calls upon corporations to act as good corporate citizens and put the welfare of society as a whole over their need to make individual profit. There are calls for a shift from the "Shareholder Model" to the "Stakeholder Model," a shift away from focusing solely on the return only for shareholders to a wider picture that focuses on the needs of all stakeholders: employees, customers, suppliers, and society at large. There is even a call towards Conscious Leadership, which asks the leaders of our corporations to move to a higher level of consciousness, taking into account the "bigger, even moral picture" when making key strategic decisions.[8]

I do not oppose any of these movements; in fact I endorse all of them. But I do not feel they will be very successful in bringing about the fundamental change necessary for the 21st century. Each of these laudable ideas fails to provide the necessary framework that will allow for wide-scale adoption and a fundamental shift in worldviews. Within the worldview of the Machine of Production, how can you possible achieve a Socially Responsible corporation? Machines are not, in fact cannot be, socially or morally responsible. Until we change the fundamental paradigm, we cannot get there. And to date the dominant justification for the changes in behavior is a call to a higher purpose. "Do Good for Good's sake and you will profit."

I believe this is true and there is a fair amount of anecdotal evidence for it. But why, why does doing good produce results? This is the question that calls for an answer. Organization leaders deserve to know that a new model is based on sound principles and better explains the world around them. Leaders have a right to expect a new model will provide the necessary tools and enable them to achieve better results than the model they currently use to produce success.

To date challenges to the "machine of production" paradigm rely on anecdotal evidence. While much of the anecdotal evidence does imply positive results as in books like *Good to Great* and *Firms of Endearment*, they do not give a roadmap for success. They explain the attributes exhibited by successful companies but do not explain why those attributes create success. They simply ask each manager to do what others have done and to take a leap of faith that such a course of action will produce better results, eventually.

While I completely agree with their premise and their promise, the promise alone will not shift the paradigm. Yes, I have been personally swayed and accept as true their premise. This is because over the course of my life, I have experienced the successes created by following those principles outlined in their books. I also recognize that for those who have not yet experienced the positive impact of these principles, accepting them requires a leap of faith in the absence of a reasonable and rational explanation of why it works. For most organizational leaders trying to address today's ever-complex challenges, the leap of faith is too great.

To quote from an August 23, 2010 article in the *Wall Street Journal*, "The Case Against Corporate Social Responsibility,"

Can companies do well by doing good? Yes—sometimes.

But the idea that companies have a responsibility to act in the public interest and will profit from doing so is fundamentally flawed.

Large companies now routinely claim that they aren't in business just for the profits, that they're also intent on serving some larger social purpose. They trumpet their efforts to produce healthier foods or more fuel-efficient vehicles, conserve energy and other resources in their operations, or otherwise make the world a better place. Influential institutions like the Academy of Management and the United Nations, among many others, encourage companies to pursue such strategies.

It's not surprising that this idea has won over so many people—it's a very appealing proposition. You can have your cake and eat it too!

But it's an illusion, and a potentially dangerous one.

Very simply, in cases where private profits and public interests are aligned, the idea of corporate social responsibility is irrelevant: Companies that simply do everything they can to boost profits will end up increasing social welfare. In circumstances in which profits and social welfare are in direct opposition, an appeal to corporate social responsibility will almost always be ineffective because executives are unlikely to act voluntarily in the public interest and against shareholder interests.[9]

Nor should they unless, as the journalist states, acting in the social good can in fact be shown to be good for the corporation. But does it have to be one or the other? Will corporate responsibility always run counter to the company's core purpose? Or is there a model of the corporation that demonstrates, in real and practical terms, that being a caring and cooperative member of society does in fact produce the greatest return to the investors? Is there a model that can reveal how these two objectives can become complimentary instead of antagonistic partners to improve productivity, profitability and new possibilities?

To begin to explain how our current machine paradigm limits our ability to see beyond the conflicting options let's look at the nature of machines. Machines have no other purpose than to produce something in the most efficient way possible. They don't care what the result is so long as it achieves that result efficiently and profitably. A machine is merely programmed to do what it is told. That's the fundamental problem with our current business paradigm. We've allowed corporations to turn into mindless machines that only do what the shareholders, the marketplace or the market manipulators, the speculators and government regulators, tell them to do. Since the 1980s, the only objective for most corporations has been to maximize shareholder value. And this they've done, as all machines do, as efficiently as possible.

But in our expanded worldview, where corporations are viewed as living beings, we can see that the best results come not from outside our organizations but from deep within them. They have within them, from their moment of creation or birth, some "purpose for being." Like every living being, The Living Organization® wants to see its purpose realized. It wants to make its mark, fulfill its purpose and maximize its contributions to the customers it serves. Living organisms, and organizations, are in a relationship with their environment. They recognize that they depend on their environment as much as their environment depends on them.

I was at a workshop at Esalen, a retreat center in the beautiful hills of Big Sur CA, overlooking the Pacific Ocean. I was invited to present The Living Organization® model to a group of Esalen managers who were exploring the next stage for their organization. After our presentations, they walked through their strategic visioning process using scenario planning as a tool to help identify possible futures. I experienced a sort of mechanical nature to the conversations as if they were going through the motions but lacked that certain spark.

I invited them to take a look at the organization not from a mental process but from a deep sense of connection with its long life. I invited them to think of Esalen as a beautiful woman that had graced many people over the years with her beauty and the magic of the location. And this beautiful woman was now forty years old and longing for a new way to contribute to the world. She was seeking a way to build on her gifts but also recognized that she was moving into the next phase of her life. This invitation changed the quality of the conversation and created new possibilities for how they could move forward. It also brought out the deep-felt passion of the management team and all the people associated with Esalen. It brought the organization new life.

Viewing our organizations as living organisms frees us from the built-in bias that arises from our limited view of corporate bodies as merely machines of production. Viewing an organization as a living entity allows us to draw from a broad range of disciplines, from physics, biology, psychology, to the many diverse spiritual traditions. Therefore we can draw on the deeper Perennial Wisdom that has guided our ability to live effective and productive lives as human beings. These same wisdoms can also guide our ability to lead our organizations' actions to effectively and productively contribute to the customers they serve and society as a whole.

What works for other living entities will work for The Living Organization®.

Wisdom of manifestation

One of those perennial wisdoms is that life is composed of dual opposites. For every up there must be a down, for black there is white. We see it everywhere, left brain thinking paired with right brain thinking, logic balanced with emotion, imagination in opposition to facts, and form juxtaposed against spirit.

Mankind's journey into a deeper understanding of how life works gave birth to the Scientific Method, the reductionist approach of Newtonian Physics. This is the societal framework on which Fredrick Taylor based his Scientific Management, part of the foundation of our current business paradigm. In this view, matter is separate from energy, or said another way, the formed physical world of existence is separate from the unformed world or the world of Spirit.

Then Einstein came along and shared his now famous equation $E=MC^2$ and changed everything. In this simple equation he points out that matter and energy are not in opposition but in fact two sides of the same coin. Matter is energy and energy is matter. He did not create the equality of matter and energy, it was always equal. He simply expanded our framework and opened the lens by which we viewed the world to reveal this complimentary relationship between what until then seemed to be polar opposites.

To understand how we can have greater impact on producing the results we want, we must understand how the physical world and the non-physical world are related. We must understand how the physical world emanates from the unmanifested energy of the non-physical fields. This is not new. It is, like Einstein, merely expanding the lens to reveal what is already present in our world.

As we said earlier, it is the very nature of life that we are always dealing with polarities; one cannot exist without the other. A coin is composed of a head and a tail. Are these opposites? From a reductionist perspective we can only see a tail or a head, one the opposite of the other. But we all know that the coin needs both the head and the tail to exist. As we expand our frame of reference from a mechanistic reductionist perspective to an organic holistic perspective, we begin to understand that what were once opposites are in fact complements, two sides of the same coin.

Just like the head and tail of the coin, complementary and balancing forces create the life we experience. Our lives are created out of these forces and are reflections of their cause and effect. Without opposites, life itself would not exist. Without science, we would be living in a world of confusion and chaos. Without spirit, we would be soul-less machines, lacking art and beauty and the creative energy needed to manifest life and the results we desire. Up-down, black-white, good-bad, science-spirit brings about the balancing of opposites that creates the wholeness of life like the head and the tail create the coin.

As with Einstein's discovery, The Living Organization® is part of an evolutionary journey. It builds on all that has come before and serves as a way of widening our lens to reveal the forces that are already present and impacting our efforts to create what we want. Life itself is a process of creation and all living entities are creative beings. Creation is the process of bringing something into form, manifesting from that which is not manifested; form from spirit, a specific result from the field of infinite possibilities.

Since everything is energy, we will continue our journey by understanding the nature of the primary material, the source of all life – energy.

CHAPTER 3

"The energy of the mind is the essence of life."
Aristotle

It's all about Energy

The transition from employee to manager was not an easy one for me. I realized that my success depended on not just my own efforts but those of everyone around me and, in particular, on my ability to orchestrate a whole new set of dynamic forces swirling around me which I couldn't see but surely felt.

I felt it in the way people reacted to me. There were times when I would think I communicated a certain message but what they received was very different. What was I sending that they were picking up that I didn't know I was sending? And why didn't I know it?

I felt it in the way results happened. Many times the teams I led produced results that were magical, like the ones at HP. Many other times the results didn't turn out nearly as expected. Yet it seemed to me I was doing the same things in both situations. I wondered what else was going on besides what I or my team was doing that yielded the results I got.

To help me through this struggle, I fell back on what I knew: my early training as a systems engineer. I found that the same principles that worked for scientifically analyzing and understanding complex physical systems worked for analyzing organizational systems as well. The deeper I delved into what was impacting my ability to accomplish my goals, the more I began to recognize that I was dealing with various forms of energy. I began to understand that creating results was all about energy and how it flowed through the system.

Results are energies transformed

The earliest known discussion of energy can be traced to the concept of "Vis Viva" or "living force" dating back to the Greek philosopher, Thales of Miletus, c625-c545 BC. We have continued to advance our understanding of the concept and properties of energy through the works of scientists and philosophers such as Gottfried Leibniz, Sir Isaac Newton, Thomas Young, William Rankin, Lord Kelvin, Albert Einstein, and many others.

The core of our current understanding is that energy is never created nor destroyed. Physicist and Nobel Laureate Richard Feynman described the law of conservation of energy in a 1961 lecture by stating:

"There is a certain quantity, which we call energy, that does not change in manifold changes which nature undergoes. That is a most abstract idea, because it is a mathematical principle. It says that there is a numerical quantity, which does not change when something happens. It is not a description of a mechanism, or anything concrete; it is just a strange fact that we can calculate some number, and when we finish watching nature go through her tricks and calculate the number again, it is the same."[10]

The sum total of all energy within any system is constant no matter what changes that system undergoes. As Einstein fully understood, everything is energy transforming from one form into another. As his predecessor Newton pointed out, energy can neither be created nor destroyed. If everything is energy, which cannot be created or destroyed, it stands to reason that creating results is a process of transforming energy from one form into the form of our desired results.

Forms of Energy

Energy has a number of attributes which we experience in different forms. Energy is visible to our five senses and also hidden from our senses. Energy takes the form of potential energy (energy waiting to express) and kinetic energy (energy expressing). Energy can take form or be in an unformed state.

Some forms of energy are relatively easy to observe while others, though known to exist, cannot be easily experienced through our five senses. A flowing river, a light beam and solid forms of energy such as a table are all easily perceived. It is also easy to observe energy in motion in the form of the actions of individuals and groups.

We can know some forms of energy because of the effect they have on something we can observe. Electricity, magnetic fields, radiation, human thoughts and even human motivations are examples of energy we cannot directly detect with our physical senses but still accept them as being present because we can witness their effects through secondary means. Electricity and radiation can be measured through instruments. Magnetic fields can be known by something as simple as observing patterns of sprinkled iron filings. Human thoughts have been recorded by MRI scanners as energy patterns and scientists can map out the regions of our brains that are responsible for different types of thoughts.

There are also flows of energy that we cannot see or even measure but accept, primarily because we experience their effects. Sensory perceptions, thoughts and emotions are all forms of energy our bodies are processing. We know energy enters our bodies through our five senses and is processed though our nervous system and our mental faculties. We also know there is a relationship between the energy generated by our thoughts and the energy felt by us as emotions.

The felt senses we call experiences are also a form of energy though they are not processed through our five physical senses. For example, watching a sunset or a baby smile will create a sensation that is a specific energy vibration. If we find ourselves in the presence of someone who is angry, without seeing or hearing them our bodies still experience and are affected by the energy they emanate. Even motivation is energy that flows through each of us, driving and defining the behaviors that all can observe.

Have you ever been in a group setting where there are unspoken issues, "the elephant in the room?" It is not the issue itself that is the felt experience but the energy that is being suppressed. Avoiding discussion of the issue blocks the energy like water behind a dam, preventing the flow of all energy and slowing work down. The minute the elephant in the room is revealed and discussed, the energy is released. Independent of the resolution of the original issue, the mere fact that the energy is again flowing creates movement. Most people who have experienced this will say they felt a certain relief that they were now discussing the issue and almost all reported an increase in energy because of this release.

From both physics and chemistry, we know that rocks at rest at the top of the hill or fuel in a gas tank are forms of unseen potential energy. Push the rock down a hill or compress the fuel in an engine and that hidden potential quickly transforms into the kinetic energy that we can observe. The same transformation of potential energy into kinetic energy can be seen in the runner poised in the blocks at the start of the race. He is potential energy that explodes into kinetic energy at the sound of the gun. Our organizations are a combination of potential energy and kinetic energy. We have a deep source of potential energy within each individual and work group just waiting to be released into the activities that will ultimately produce our desired results.

The patterns of our lives

Energy, and therefore life itself, is always in a constant state of motion. Indeed, all life is in the process of transforming from one state of energy to another. Since energy cannot be created or destroyed, one has to ask the question: Where is the energy before it becomes formed? It must reside somewhere, in a non-physical state, prior to it coming into form.

Einstein's famous equation $E=MC^2$ points out that energy waves and particle matter are the same. Vibrating energy waves flow into electrons, which flow together with protons to form atoms, atoms form molecules, molecules form cells, and so on. And from this life itself is created. All forms of life consist of energy patterns merging and mingling to form new patterns, not unlike the patterns of rabbits, turtles, and dragons a child (and some adults) can see in the moving, flowing clouds.

Just as clouds form from less dense, unformed water vapor into the denser form that allow us to discern the various patterns, all energy moves from less dense, unformed, subtle energy to the more dense formed energy of our physical world. All energy continuously moves and morphs from one pattern into another and then dissipates back into the unmanifested field of energy. Whether the energy patterns are dense enough to be observable or not, the energy is still present and potentially impacting us.

People Are Energy Too

If matter emerges from energy, then people must also be a form of energy. We can best be understood as patterns of energy that coalesce as DNA, cells, organs, tissue, and muscle into our unique form and body. In addition to energy fashioning itself into the form of our bodies, energy runs through our bodies in other forms such as thoughts, desires, emotions, and experience. We may not always think of these aspects of ourselves as less dense forms of energy. But that is what they are.

We speak of an individual as exhibiting certain traits or behavior patterns. These are also patterns of energy being expressed. Thoughts and emotions are energy patterns, less obvious perhaps, but just as real. Though they may not be observable in the physical world, they do exist and to a large degree contribute to the creation of our physical world.

Allow yourself for a moment to feel love for someone. Allow that feeling to rise in intensity and fill your whole body. Do this for a moment and then begin to pay attention to your body. How would you describe what you are feeling at this moment? Most people will respond with feelings of calm, peace, warmth, and settlement.

Now take another moment and allow yourself to remember a time when you were angry at someone or some situation. Bring that situation to mind as fully as possible. Allow the anger to rise up within you to fill your body as fully as you can. Again reflect on how your body feels. In these situations most people would respond that the body is wound up as tight as a drum, fuming, and red hot.

In each case your body is vibrating to a certain energy frequency. Love is an energy vibration whereby all the component parts of the body's organization, muscles, and cells attune to and create the experience of relaxation, calm, and peace. The opposite is true of anger, which is a specific vibration that attunes all the bodily components to a different frequency. These emotions and the states they produce are patterns of energy.

I have used a similar exercise with groups in management training. The biggest challenges most managers and executives have is keeping up with the long list of tasks they have to work through. They have reports to get in on time, performance reviews they have to do, customers they have to meet, meetings to attend, planning to finish, and the list goes on and on. In my exercise I have them make a list of all the tasks they had to get done within the next 5 – 10 days. The list was to start with "I have to - _____ by _____." Then I have them pick a partner and read their lists to each other. At the end I ask them to describe the feelings they had in their bodies. Tired, heavy, burdened, and overwhelmed are typical responses I get. Then I have them take the same list, change the opening phrase from "I have to" to "I want to" or alternatively "I get to." I then have them read their list again to their partner and record the way their bodies felt. Excited, energized, and uplifted are some of the common responses.

The activities on both lists were the same. All that changed was two words: "Have to" with "Want to." Words are associated with beliefs. "Have to" is associated with obligation, while "want to" is associated with choice. Obligation carries a different energy frequency than the frequency of choice and the experiences we have are directly related to these different patterns of energy in our bodies.

Choice lets energy flow

On a visit to the Santa Clara office of HP, the Area General Manager and the Branch manager shared with me a challenge they were having with a particular employee. Chris was part of the lease contract administration group. He was extremely talented, very sharp, and was creating wonderful programs that helped streamline the administrative process. However, Chris was not carrying his load in terms of managing the lease contracts. Every time they talked with him, he would promise to do what was expected and did for a while but then would slack off again. They tried everything they could to get him back on track and asked if I would talk with Chris.

I asked Chris if he knew why we were getting together. He clearly understood the problem. He explained to me that he really felt that what he was doing, developing the software to make the process more efficient, was making a great contribution to not only his department but also to the overall region. I acknowledged the value of what he was doing and his love for programming. I also told him that what he was doing was not the job we hired him to do. That while he was working on developing the software, which would have a payback for the future, the day to day work of administering the contracts was falling on the shoulders of his team members.

"But in the long run it will reduce the workload of everyone," he said.

"Yes, that is true," I said, "and as with all things I have to balance the long term against the short term. What you want to do falls into the category of future investments."

"But don't you see how much of a difference I am making?"

"Yes, of course I do," I said. "But that is not one of the choices I have available for you. If we allow you to continue on as you are, then we will have to hire someone else to do the work you were hired for, move you into the IT department and adjust our priorities to pay for your efforts. From the bigger picture, that is not an option I want to support."

At first, I could see from his expression that he felt boxed in, trapped and cornered. I followed up by acknowledging his love for programming. "Chris, I can tell you really love to program and to use your talents to improve organizational effectiveness. I think that is a real gift. Unfortunately that is not an option I have available to you at this point. What we have is the position we hired you to do and we all know you have the talent to do it. What do you want to do?"

He thought for a moment and then shared how a friend of his had offered him an opportunity to work with him in his startup, developing software for their internal processes. As he described the position he began to get really excited, his eyes lit up and he started to connect with something he really loved. It was obvious there was a tremendous amount of energy flowing.

"Chris," I said, "you seem really excited about this opportunity. You light up with such a sense of excitement and passion. Why don't you take that job?"

Again Chris was quiet for a moment and then he said, "You are right. That is what excites me." Chris decided to resign that day and take the opportunity to do what he really wanted to do.

For months my managers tried hard to get Chris to do what they needed him to do and tried all sorts of ways to motivate him to do it. What they never did was make it Chris's choice. A simple act of laying out the options and offering the choice empowers employees more than any attempt to motivate desired behavior. Choice allows energy to flow and as it is flowing, it can be directed towards the desired results. As discovered in the earlier "Have To/Want To" exercise, feeling that you have to do something blocks the flow of energy. And wishing you had a different option than what is available will also block the flow of energy and slow down or even prevent the creation of desired results.

Everything is energy! As these examples demonstrate, we are constantly responding to energy with energy. One can consider life as nothing but a mysterious dance of interacting and exchanging energy.

The Dance of energy

It is not just the energy that flows within us that creates our experience, it is the energy that surrounds us as well. Energy flows into patterns or energy fields that are in relationship, constantly interacting with each other. All entities in any relationship have the characteristic of simultaneously impacting and being impacted by the interaction of those entities.

When you interact with another person, you impact them and they impact you, positively or negatively. As we breathe, we expel carbon dioxide and take in oxygen. We interact with our environment, specifically trees and plants that take in carbon dioxide and give off oxygen.

We live in a sea of different energy patterns and each pattern, depending on the strength of the field, will have a direct impact on our experience, especially if we are not aware of its influence.

One of my clients is a $25 million software company in Southern California that had been struggling to better align the executive team. While there was conflict among many of the team members, there was a specific conflict between the VP of Marketing and the VP of Sales, which was affecting the company's ability to meet their growth strategies. During one of my coaching meetings with the VP of Marketing, he shared his most recent upset with the VP of Sales. The two of them met with the CEO and both agreed to take on certain tasks and have them completed by a certain date. The VP of Marketing saw signs that the VP of Sales might miss that date and sent an email, copying the CEO, calling out the VP of Sales for falling behind and predicting that the commitment would not be met.

The VP of Marketing had only been with the company a few months and this behavior was not consistent with his normal style of team interactions. I asked why he communicated that way he had. His answer was, "We agreed to something and he was not going to come through."

"Why did you do it in an email and copy the CEO?" I asked.

"It was a commitment we had agreed to in a meeting amongst the three of us."

"Are you guys on the same team?" I asked.

"Yes, of course we are," he said.

"I don't know about you," I said. "But when I see a teammate getting into trouble I don't call him out in front of our boss in a formal medium like an email. Instead I reach out to see if I can help. I usually pick up the phone and call him and ask if he needs any help or if he thinks it will still get done on time."

The VP of Marketing stopped for a moment, reflected on his behavior and said, "I don't know why I did that. I know better."

Why did he behave in a way that is contrary to what he knows? The answer again is energy, in this case the collective energy field, or pattern, of the organization's culture. To give you a deeper insight, it was very common for the executives to compete for the favor of the CEO to an excessive degree in this culture. They took every opportunity to throw members of their team under the bus if they could blame them and shine in the eyes of the CEO. This was one of the reasons we were brought into to the organization, to help transform their culture and the dynamics of the executive team. It took less than three months for this new executive, who in all of his previous positions had never acted this way, to take on the energy pattern of the team and begin to behave just like everyone else.

This is but one example of the power of energy, of energy forces impacting every organization's ability to create results, energy forces that all too often remain under the surface of leadership's awareness. This book and the ones to follow are intended to help you understand these forces and how to work with them to your advantage.

Energy patterns that create are alive

All of life is energy but not all energy is alive. A table is energy but a table is not alive. Water is energy that takes many forms but not many people will say water is alive, though it has life-giving properties. Lava is energy but it usually is not considered to be alive. It may change states in relation to its environment from molten lava to solid lava but it is still lava.

Energy patterns that form living organisms not only have their own energy transformed; they transform the energy of other energy fields. They in essence create. Creation is what differentiates energy that is alive from other forms of energy. Plants are alive, humans are alive and organizations are alive.

Living energy patterns interact and co-create with their environment. Plants take in carbon dioxide and turn that into oxygen, which they give off for animals to breathe. They also absorb nutrients from the soil and transform them into the sugars and fibers which animals take in to grow muscles and fuel movement. Like plants, humans also take in many forms of energy and transform them into other forms in continuing acts of creation.

All living organisms create by transforming energy from one form into another. All living organisms interact with their environment, impacting and being impacted as the two co-create. As humans, however, we have an additional energy field that is part of our creation process: desire and intention. We choose what we want to create.

Energy at a rate of over 50,000 thoughts passes through our brains every day[11]. We pay little attention to most of these energy patterns but a select few catch our attention and are repeated over and over again. These thoughts become slightly more coalesced in the form we call a belief. When we charge the belief with the energy of emotion and continue to flow more and more energy to it, that belief becomes our paradigm, defining the way the world works for us. We also filter what we think is possible to create by our belief systems, our worldviews. From this paradigm we take action in response to our environment to manifest our intentions and desires.

We are patterns of energy in relationship, flowing and interacting with other patterns of energy, creating and evolving. This is how we create our physical world experiences and the results we experience.

The Evolutionary Flow of Energy

Evolution is a process in which life adds onto and expands that which came before, where one life form joins with others to form more complex life forms. It is from these interactions that life has evolved over many millennia and from which a new form of life, "the organization," continues to evolve.

I will leave to the philosophers, scientists, theologians and others to debate whether evolution occurs by intelligent design or by random acts of nature. What we do know is that everywhere we look life evolves from simple forms into more complex forms. Electrons bind with protons and together they form atoms, the foundation of matter. Atoms come together to form molecules, molecules form compounds, and so on.

In his book *Biology of Beliefs*, Bruce Lipton explains this from the point of view of a microbiologist.

It shouldn't be surprising that cells are so smart. Single-celled organisms were the first life forms on this planet...initially only free-living, single celled organisms – bacteria, algae and amoeba-like protozoa – populated the world.

Before 750 million years ago, these smart cells figured out how to get smarter when the first multi-cellular organisms (plants, fish and later animals) appeared. Multi-cellular life forms were initially loose communities or "colonies" of single-celled organisms. At first, cellular communities consisted of tens and hundreds of cells. But the evolutionary advantage of living in a community led to organizations comprised of millions, billions and even trillions of socially interactive cells... While the cellular communities appear as single entities to the naked eye – a mouse, a dog, a human – they are, in fact, highly organized associations of millions and trillions of cells.

The evolutionary push for ever-bigger communities is simply a reflection of the biological imperative to survive. The more awareness an organism has of its environment the better its chances for survival. When cells band together they increase their chances exponentially...

To survive at such high densities, the cells created structured environments. These communities subdivided the workload with more precision and effectiveness than the ever-changing organizational charts that are a fact of life in big corporations.[12]

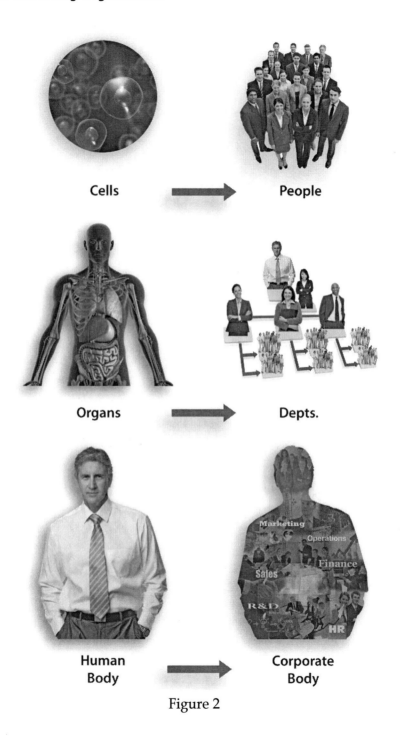

Figure 2

The nature of evolution is that fields of energy, taking the form of living organisms, evolve to higher levels of complexity and sophistication. All living forms are composed of energy fields that are in turn composed of other energy fields. Organisms are composed of other organisms. Certain organisms join together to serve a common objective, which in turn creates a higher order and a more complex purpose and energy pattern.

If we can accept that humans, the most advanced and complex form of life on this planet, are comprised of countless individual organisms that structure themselves like the organizational charts of a big corporation, then isn't it reasonable to also view corporations as highly evolved complex living beings? In fact we can easily see the parallels between the human body and the corporate body as shown in Figure 2 on the previous page.

The individuals in an organization can be viewed as the basic cellular building blocks of an organization, much like the cells in the human body. Individuals of like mind join together with other individuals for a common objective comprising another living organism we call a team. These teams form the fundamental unit of the organization, which in business we refer to as the "functional structure." The functional departments of sales, marketing, and engineering are analogous to the various organs of the human body, such as the heart, liver, and lungs.

While the human body is a complex web of energy fields flowing and interacting with each other, a human being is much more than just its body. We think, feel, have experiences, pose intuitive insights and are self-aware. We are aware of an inner self and the complex web of inner voices that guide us through life, some of which are in opposition to each other. We are also aware of our outer selves and our interactions with others. The same is true for The Living Organization®. And it doesn't stop there

If we use The Living Organization® as the starting point, we see that markets consist of groups of such organisms – companies, competitors, consumers - coming together to serve a common goal, all within a larger entity or market. From there, markets form societies, societies form our planet, and on it goes.

Like the Russian dolls that neatly fit one within the other, The Living Organizations® carry within them other living organizations. They in fact demonstrate the fractal property of self-similarity; the rules of energy that apply to one living organization apply to all living organizations. The laws, rules, and methods that we will describe in this book apply equally to the results created by an individual, a group, a team, a department, and to an organization.

For the purposes of this book, we will stick with the single entity, The Living Organization®, and show how applying the laws of energy provides a new, more effective framework for breathing life back into any organization.

CHAPTER 4

> *"An organization's ability to learn, and translate that learning into action rapidly, is the ultimate competitive advantage."* **Jack Welch**

The Energy of Business

All companies and organizations are composed of a multitude of individuals who form into groups to form an even more complex system. All complex living systems, whether an individual or an organization, consist of energy fields beyond the obvious ones that make up the physical "body." These subtler energy fields are the thoughts, beliefs, emotions, passions and deeper purpose that guide the choices and behaviors of living systems. As a living organization, your company must also carry within it these subtler energy fields, including the energy of its Soulful Purpose™ (which we will discuss in greater detail later).

All living things come into existence for specific reasons, to be an expression of this deeper purpose. Pure randomness or accident does not bring such a diverse array of energy patterns together to form a living entity. The Soulful Purpose™ is a powerful force attracting the right energy patterns to engage and realize its mission. An acorn is born to become an oak, a liver cell serves to become part of the liver, heart cells become part of a heart, and heart and liver become part of the body. Each living entity has a unique reason for existing, a unique contribution to make to something greater than itself.

The same is true for The Living Organization® as it attracts people to it to serve its Soulful Purpose™ and realize its mission. There is an attractive force that brings certain people to certain companies. We can see this most visibly in entrepreneurial start ups where the reason people join that particular organization is because of the alignment with its Soulful Purpose™. And like the way cells organize within the human body, people come together to form teams, teams form departments, and departments form companies. All come together to contribute their individual and collective energy which is transformed into the collectively desired results that serves something greater than itself.

Are you attracting the right people? Is your Soulful Purpose™ known and felt? IS the reason you exist to serve something greater than yourself? Is your organization a Living Organization®?

The Flow

Energy flows on a defined path through every living organism. This path is designed to maximize the transformation of energy from its source into the form of its desired outcomes. Similarly there is a defined path of energy flowing through an organization and the goal is to maximize the transformation of energy from its source to its desired outcome.

The purpose of every company is to provide products and services that are perceived as valuable and are highly desired by the customers they serve, as shown in Figure 3. Simply put, the output of the business-system is the goods and services that allow us to serve our customers.

Figure 3

To achieve this result, you must transform energy from a source into the goods and services you provide to the customer. The source of energy, the starting point for the transformational process, is the people who make up your company and who give form and substance to the thoughts, ideas, and ambitions of the organization. Each person is a source of energy.

Contrary to the view that people are interchangeable, every individual in The Living Organization® has a unique set of gifts to contribute and a special role to play. Just as no two snowflakes are alike, no two people are alike. We have numerous traits that are similar, we have very similar skills, but we will never be exactly the same. Each person brings a unique perspective, insight and expression to the work they do, work that is the transformation of energy in a process we call creation.

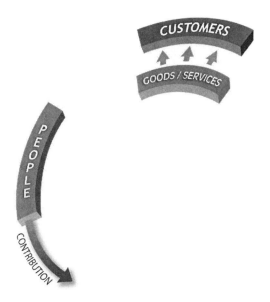

Figure 4

As shown in Figure 4, through the conscious, active release of energy from people contributing to the common objective, we derive the major energy source for the transformative process we call production.

If we expect to transform people's energy into our desired output, we must direct and focus their free-flowing energy toward a common outcome. Getting a group of people together to be "active" would produce a lot of energy but not necessarily a useful result. The transformation of their efforts into the goods and services customers crave and value would not occur. Active but unfocused groups produce undirected states of diffused energy that soon dissipate.

Think of this like a beam of light. A standard light bulb releases energy into the room that spreads in a highly diffused manner. This is good if you want to illuminate the entire room. If your objective were to use the light to cut through a wall, an ordinary light bulb is of little value. However, when we focus the light energy into a laser beam, we transform it into a concentrated form of energy which can easily cut through walls.

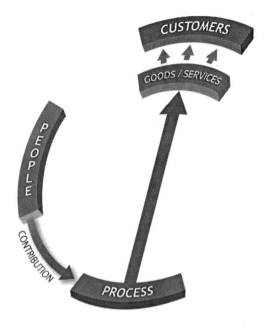

Figure 5

Rarely do we find groups of people being active for activity's sake, yet almost everyone has an experience of a group of people doing things in uncoordinated, diffused ways. For example, a multinational internet security company asked us to help improve sales growth. We determined that the sales team was extremely passionate and fully committed to achieving their goals, but lacked structure to their efforts. There was a tremendous amount of contributed energy but little in the way of organizing their combined efforts. Territory assignments made no sense. Sales people followed their leads as best they could. There was no well designed sales process so each sales person created their own. Each had a different definition of where they were in the sales process and a different way of forecasting the likelihood of closing a sale. You can imagine the chaos that swirled around not only the sales team, but the rest of the organization as well. Sales people were in constant conflict over who owned the opportunity. Engineering kept getting pulled into "critical" sales opportunities and manufacturing could not forecast production demands accurately their.

High levels of energy are critical but not sufficient. As the example above illustrates without the structure of appropriately designed business processes there will be a tremendous energy loss through the system. Business processes are the energy waveguides coordinating the efforts, the contribution energy, of our people as shown in Figure 5 on the previous page.

In a complex system there are multiple groups of living entities whose energy not only must be directed but integrated with each other's energy contribution. In our example above the sales efforts need to coordinate with engineering and manufacturing. An organization is comprised of individuals contributing their own energy and of individuals working together as teams. These collaborative teams exchange energy with one another to collectively achieve the organization's goals.

Business processes also serve to integrate the different sources of energy into one powerful force that can move mountains or cut through walls. They are designed to integrate the flow of energy from the marketing group so it is in phase with the flow of energy from sales. Properly designed processes will mix sales energy with operations and engineering until a total transformation takes place and the process creates value. This is how energy flows through the system we call business.

Though it often feels complex, you can keep everything in perspective if you understand it simply as flows of energy that come from the efforts of the people, guided and directed by a common purpose into a focused source like a laser beam. The internal business processes guide the energy flow of The Living Organization®, directing, aligning, integrating and transforming the "people power" into the goods and services desired by your customers.

However, processes cut both ways. They are critical to coordinating, integrating and focusing energy and they have a tendency to get bloated and inefficient. We have all dealt with organizations where the rules of interaction override the purpose of the interaction. We call this bureaucracy. We usually associate it with government agencies but our companies can get bogged down in bureaucratic malaise as well. We have rules for rules sake. Instead of people making decisions based on situational conditions, they must follow the policy.

Think of the last time you called customer support for help that required some deviation from the standard procedure. All too often you can forget getting any resolution. Even if you go up the chain to the supervisor, the typical response is, "Sorry sir that is all we can do for you." If they are honest they will sometimes say, 'Sorry sir, this is our policy and we do not have the authority to do anything else."

Sometimes our business process is adjusted to incorporate new situations that have come up from time to time. New rules are laid on top of existing rules and over time we end up with a series of workflow processes and rules that makes no sense. We do what we do because that is how it has always been done. This bloat generates a lot of friction and loss of energy. Over the last three decades, many companies have attempted to systematically reduce the loss of energy through the transformation process. Programs such as Total Quality Management, Six Sigma and Process Reengineering are all designed to streamline the business processes used to guide the flow of energy, which reduces wasted energy.

The Source of All Energy: Our People

Maximizing the flow of energy through the system by reducing energy loss has been the primary focus for organizations since the 1970s. Some might argue since the beginning of the modern corporation. However, little was done to address increasing the energy at its source, the people who fuel the transformation process.

As organizations grow, they add people. This increases the supply of energy available for the company to transform into the goods and services for their customers. However, adding people is the least effective way to increase the amount of energy available. Not only does it add costs such as labor and overhead, it adds additional complexity since more people require more coordination.

A better way to increase the amount of energy flowing through the system is to significantly increase the amount of energy at the source, the amount of energy contributed by each employee.

The unique quality of people, unlike other sources of energy, is that the energy people can contribute is infinitely renewable. Humans have demonstrated that their capacity to contribute energy does not deplete but can be recharged very quickly. As an energy source, people exhibit another unique quality: their ability to contribute energy can actually expand. Individuals can grow their capacity to contribute increasing amounts of energy.

This is a fascinating part of this new model – the primary source of energy, the people within The Living Organization®, can increase their capacity to draw on a nearly inexhaustible reserve of potential energy. They are a conduit to an almost endless storehouse of energy, both physical and mental, and a fountain of creative contributions to the life and productivity of their collective, corporate body.

I have been involved with a variety of non-profits for over 20 years and am currently the chairman of two of them. I have always been amazed by how much energy people who volunteer for non-profits bring to their efforts. Think about it. These are the same people who leave work drained and exhausted, feeling the drudgery of their day-to-day efforts to eke out a living. They leave work and head over to volunteer at their chosen non-profit. Within the blink of an eye, they are transformed. They become excited and filled with an energy that is enlivening. Where does that energy come from? What magical source have they tapped into? Wouldn't you like to have your employees apply that same level of energy to their work to create results for your corporation? In this book and the ones that follow, you will learn how to create the conditions that open your employee's access to that deep well of energy.

We don't know the limits of human development. We do know that when people learn and grow, they expand their capability to access and use energy to contribute to their success. Learning improves our skills, which allows us to do our task more efficiently. Learning is the ability to improve one's effectiveness, the ability to get the desired results with the least amount of effort. Growth is the ability to increase the amount of energy a person has available to contribute. People as an energy source are infinitely renewable, infinitely expandable, and can learn to apply their energy highly efficiently.

We include "learning" as a critical component of the flow of energy in our model in Figure 6 on the next page.

There is also, as you can observe in the model, a relationship between *contribution* and *learning*. To learn something, we must accomplish something we don't already know how to do. It could be learning to do a brand new task or learning new ways to do a task we already do but want to do better. In either case putting forth an effort towards a goal (contributing our energy) is a prerequisite for learning to happen. As we said, when we learn we have more energy to contribute to our efforts, which creates the contribution-learning cycle.

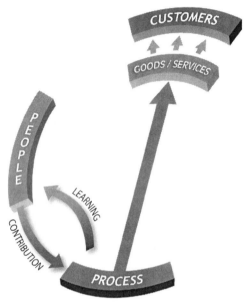

Figure 6

Increasing the energy contribution of each employee is the same as increasing employee productivity, a common goal in any organization. Most efforts at productivity improvement have been oriented around providing energy enhancers or leverage as opposed to creating a contribution-learning cycle. For example, tools from the simplest machinery to more complex computers and robotics all leverage the efforts of each employee, providing greater output for the same amount of energy contributed.

But too often leveraging energy with tools is where we stop. Learning and growth represent more than just leveraging existing energy: they represent an actual increase in the energy contributed. As we said earlier, growth increases the amount of energy available to a person while learning provides the improved skills to use that energy more effectively. This combination of learning and growth has the multiplier effect of making more energy available and using it more effectively. And if you then add the leverage of tools you further multiply the increase of energy flowing through the system. The end result: more gets done with less.

CHAPTER 5

> *"Prosperity should never be an end in itself, but merely a means to some wholesome purpose."*
> **Buddha**

Profit: The Good, Bad and Ugly

The Need for Feedback

Every engineer knows that all systems require feedback to ensure that they are operating properly. Every working system is designed with a "feedback loop" to measure actual output, comparing that which is created to what is desired. This allows the system, and those monitoring it, to make necessary adjustments.

For business, this feedback loop is the financial system, shown in Figure 7 on the next page, which we use to measure the successful achievement of our goals. The financial system is a well-developed system of metrics that provides insight into business performance. Using the common, well-understood gauge of money, we have a tangible way to measure success. If our business is out of balance and not performing in accord with the marketplace, the gauge of our business system, our "corporate checkbook" will get out of balance as well.

Proper use of financial metrics can provide critical feedback from the market and insight into where corrections are needed.

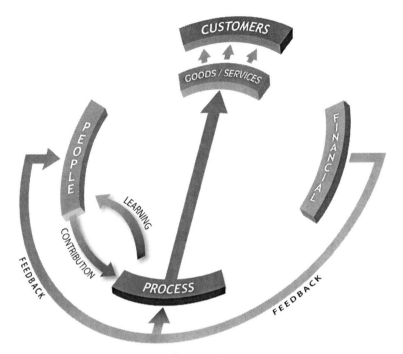

Figure 7

Without financial systems, companies would be rudderless: they could not make the necessary adjustments to ensure the system is achieving the desired outcomes.

Profit is the core metric providing feedback on the performance of the system, the gauge we rely on to give us critical information on how well the system is performing. But wait, you ask. We've been talking about the transformation of energy from the source, our people, to the delivery of goods and services to the market. How does money fit into energy transformation?

Money is simply another form of energy. Think of how economists view and work with money. They discuss the supply of money and the velocity of money in much the same way a physicist will discuss the supply of energy and the velocity of energy in the system they are studying. In fact there is a school of economics known as thermoeconomics that uses the same equations as thermodynamics to understand the economy.

Thermoeconomics is based on the proposition that the role of energy in evolution should be defined and understood through the second law of thermodynamics. And such economic criteria as productivity, efficiency, and especially the costs and benefits (or profitability) should be understood as various mechanisms for capturing and utilizing available energy. Thermoeconomists claim that human economic systems can be modeled as thermodynamic systems.[13]

Remember, the first law of thermodynamics says that energy cannot be created or destroyed. In the flow of business, we convert the energy of the people into goods and services which are purchased by a customer, who pays for it with a unit of energy we call money. This exchange of energy, in the form of money, is used to pay our employees and vendors, whose energy is converted into the energy that represents the goods and services we sell to customers. The cycle repeats and is the flow that energizes business.

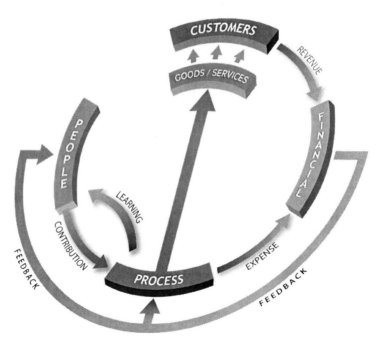

Figure 8

The Nature of Profit

Although some consider profit "the root of all evil," it is anything but that. Profit is the foundational metric and a critically important component of the feedback loop. It provides information on the state of the balance between two other key metrics – revenue and expenses. Let's look at profit in a little more detail, specifically its two main components, revenue and expenses, shown in Figure 8 on the previous page, and see how when used properly they provide insight and feedback on system performance towards its goal of serving customers and society.

As we said, selling your product is simply another transformation of energy, the exchange of the product for payment. The sum of all such conversions is the metric we call revenue. Revenue measures the marketplace's perceived value of our organization's goods and services. The higher the perceived value and the larger number of members of the market that perceive that value, the more energy we receive and the more our corporate body will grow.

The second component of the profit equation is expenses. Expenses are simply the measure of how energy (primarily labor and materials) is used in the transformation into goods and services. Expenses are an exact measurement of how efficiently energy is transformed on into the products and services the market perceives as valuable.

Profit is the metric that informs The Living Organization® about the degree to which the market perceives value in the goods and services we collectively produce in relationship to the energy consumed to produce them. Profit equals the sum total of the perceived value of goods and services less the energy consumed to produce those goods and services.

Without a proper gauge to provide the necessary feedback, a system can get "out of whack," oscillate out of control and eventually fail. However, as important as profit and the rest of our financial system is to the success of our business, it is only the feedback on the goal: it is not the goal itself. When the focus turns to money as the goal, our decisions become oriented towards the maximization of profits without realizing what drives profit. We lose sight of why we are in business.

Obsessing over profit or viewing it as the Soulful Purpose™ of an organization's existence is not only misguided but dangerous. This is when profit, and dare I say capitalism itself, begins to be viewed as the root of all our societies woes. The blind pursuit of profit, the desire to achieve profit for its own sake, is what has caused most of the greatest calamities we've experienced in business and society as a whole (particularly the near collapse of our financial system in 2009). To achieve profit at all costs, we employ the skills of financial engineers to adjust the gauge rather than improve the performance of the operation, often at the expense of the business itself and society at large.

Knowing I was a long term executive with Hewlett Packard, many people ask me how I feel about what has happened to HP over the last few years. I can only answer by expressing the great sadness I feel. While I have not been involved with the company for over two decades, the positive impact my time with HP has had on my life and many of the lessons I learned have laid the foundation for my current success. Beyond that, HP once stood for something and the employees felt the pride of belonging to an organization that we considered one of the best companies to work for. The HP Way meant something deep to all of us who had the pleasure of working there.

The greatest sadness comes from realizing that its troubles stem from the company losing its way. It lost connection with its soul, that which made it the unique being that so many looked up to. How did that happen? Since I was not with the company during those times, I can only report from the outside. I observed that the company shifted from standing for something deep and meaningful to defining itself purely by profit. Carly Fiorina came in as CEO with her number one goal to grow the company.

I remember their ad campaign featuring the old garage and the use of the Tagline "Invent" as an attempt to reignite their original sense of purpose and meaning, but it was all words and no meaning. The real message was "we are going to grow for growth's sake" and they did. Carly put together a very large merger, which many felt was a disastrous mistake and which led to a major boardroom battle. Carly won and the merger happened. It wasn't long before the company realized that she was not getting the job done and replaced her.

In came Mark Hurd, who everyone thought would restore HP to its original glory. At first it appeared he might actually do that. He improved the bottom line very quickly and from the outside, looking only at the traditional metrics of profit, he appeared to be succeeding. Then the real story emerged. From friends who were still close to the company, I learned that Mark achieved this, in part, by cutting the R&D budget, the very lifeblood that made HP great. Traditionally HP allocated 10% of its annual budget to R&D, an investment that allowed it to fulfill its Soulful Purpose™ of contributing advances in the fields it engaged in. "Making valuable contributions to the fields we engaged in" was one of the core principles in its stated objectives when I was with HP and the commitment to R&D was the way we demonstrated that commitment. Under Mark, the R&D budget was cut to less than 2%. He increased profits but what did he sacrifice?

For me, watching the collapse of this once great icon is like watching the fall from grace of many of our once great leaders, the lies of the Watergate scandal leading to the resignation of President Nixon, the steroid scandals that have brought down so many of our sports heroes, and the many scandals we have experienced over the last decade in the business community - Enron, Adelphia, Madoff, to name just a few. Is the chase for profit for profit's sake worth the price we pay as a society? I think not.

How did we get here? If profit is the principal gauge of your firm's feedback loop and you as a manager don't like the reading, you face two alternatives. One, you can adjust the way you do things and change course. Or you can adjust the gauge to receive the readings that make you look good to the outside world.

The later might sound silly—indeed it is extremely silly and even dangerous—but this is what many financial engineers have helped us do over the past decade. It can take many forms. Off-balance-sheet financing employed by Enron is one such manipulation that distorts the indication shown on the profit meter. Another is the clever creation of credit default swaps and other financial instruments that cloud our ability to obtain accurate readings from the gauge. The many finance institutions that created these clever financial engineering tools like Lehman Brothers, Bear Stearns, and Goldman Sachs packaged groups of assets and presented them as valuable. They did so by obfuscating the true underlying value of the assets while giving a false sense of security to the asset. This financial engineering improved the reading on our financial gauge without paying attention to improving the system being measured.

I do not want to imply that all financial engineering is bad. The very practice began in a sincere attempt to help companies gain access to the capital they needed to grow and serve their customers. After all the financial structure of an organization helps firms find the optimal balance among the many forms of energy they use..

The single most debilitating blow to our corporate society came when we elevated profit over creating value for customers. This accelerated the emergence of the dark side of business. "Greed is Good" became the underlying theme although it was dressed in different clothes: maximizing shareholder value. As a result, we directed the creative energy of financial engineering towards adjusting the gauge over organizational engineering to improve underlying performance.

Ensuring that the investors in a corporation receive a good return for their investment has always been an important goal for every company. Without a reasonable return, it would not be able to attract investors to their company, depriving it of needed growth capital. In the early eighties, the goal of an organization to "maximize shareholder value" elevated the bottom line to almost deity status. This is often attributed to Jack Welch, then CEO of General Electric Corporation, and his presentation to GE shareholders at their annual meeting. Yet nowhere in that presentation does Mr. Welch ever say that maximizing shareholder value is the sole or even key goal for a company. In fact, in a March 2009 interview, Mr. Welch acknowledged that this idea was carried to extremes when he said, "On the face of it, shareholder value is the dumbest idea in the world. Shareholder value is a result, not a strategy."[14]

Perhaps it was the investment community that decided that what Jack said meant he was going to maximize shareholder value because that is what served their purpose the best. Or perhaps it was just the time and mood of our society that the investor, who by that point in time became you and me and everyone who had 401ks and mutual funds, wanted to see our returns grow no matter what.

There are far too many examples of the consequences of this shift in focus. In 1986 Ivan Boesky was convicted of insider trading. In 1989 Michael Milken was convicted in the junk bond scandal and Charles

Keating in the savings and loan debacle. In 2001 we had the Enron scandal, in 2002 WorldCom and Tyco, 2008 brought the revelation of Madoff's Ponzi scheme and the collapse of the sub-prime market burst the housing bubble and led to the great recession. I am not saying that such misconduct is new to the world of business or any other area of society, but it is striking how much has occurred since the 1980s when the focus on maximizing shareholder value elevated profit from a metric that helps guide our decisions to the ultimate and primary reason we are in business.

Over the last 30 years our society has moved its focus gradually but steadily away from the vision of the founders of most of our corporations. Many company founders understand that the true purpose, power and importance of the company reside in its potential to make valued and transformative contributions to society. Clearly it is not the purpose and role of corporations to simply be profit machines.

This shift to maximizing profit as the end unto itself, as opposed to seeing it as a measure for system feedback, is the fundamental reason why the word corporation has such a negative connotation, why businesses and the CEOs who lead them are viewed with such disdain by the media and government, and why our society is struggling to right the "listing ship of commerce."

When I was an executive with Hewlett Packard we, like every corporation, went through an annual review of our strategy and future development plans. This review focused on what we could do to better serve our customers as the primary objective. Profit goals were a critical metric which we used as a way to know we were achieving our objectives and generating the resources to fund our growth.

But read most strategic plans today and they will invariably have as their number one objective, "grow revenues and profits." And why shouldn't they? It is the dominant societal pattern and, as the ocean's current pushes the iceberg, the "profit motif current pushes us. It has become the mantra of our society, "the bottom line of business is the bottom line," and who is going to argue against it. It is also very tangible and easy to measure. Trying to articulate a sense of meaning and purpose is much more difficult. We all fall prey to the power of the metric.

When I founded Quantum Leaders, I started by developing my plan for growing the company. When people asked me, "What is your vision for Quantum Leaders?" I would invariably answer, "To see my company become a $100 million consulting firm over the next 20 years." Then a dear friend asked me a frightening question, "What does it mean to become a $100 million company?" It stopped me cold. What did it mean?

Was I looking to just have millions of dollars, more money than I could possibly spend? Was it recognition, fame and glory that I sought? Or was there some other underlying drive behind my desire to grow a $100 million company?

Then I realized that the money goal was nothing more than an indication of the degree by which we would make a difference in the world. That's when I understood that my company's true goal was more than merely becoming a $100 million company. It was to make a difference, to articulate a new model that could transform businesses.

I knew that business was where many people spend the majority of their time. If we could change the way business related to its role in society, to its customers, and to its employees, we would make a very large and very real difference. That's what my life's journey has revealed to me, that is why I spent years developing and evolving this model and that is what this first book is about.

Now when I am asked what the vision of Quantum Leaders is, I say, "It is to transform business around the world into environments that *support and enhance the dignity of the human spirit as they collectively express this spirit in service to society.*"

CHAPTER 6

"And as he spoke of understanding, I looked up and saw the rainbow leap with flames of many colors over me." **Black Elk**

The Rainbow Within

Our new perspective for leaders views the organization as a living system, directing the flows of energies within that body of people and transforming their collective energy and effort into the products and services brought to the marketplace.

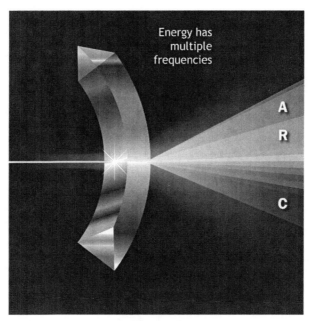

Figure 9

It follows, then, that two key components for success are to maximize energy (goods that become revenue) flowing through this living system while minimizing energy loss (expenses). That is, maximize profits. We have presented this flow of energy as a single wave, uniform in nature.

Yet it would be more accurate to think of it like the energy of light, that when passed through a prism is revealed to consist of a number of different colors, each with its own unique wavelength and frequency.

Like light energy, the flow of organizational energy is a rainbow of colors. Specifically, in Figure 9 on the previous page we see three separate waves or fields of energy: Activity, Relationship, and Context, each with its own discernable patterns, tones and operational frequencies.

Activity - the Energy of Doing

Activity

- What We Do
- Linear
- Cause & Effect
- Categorize
- Left Brain
- Mental Intelligence (IQ)

So far we have described the portion of the model that consists of the flow of energy that lies within the Activity Field. It is the energy of action, the energy of "what we do and how we do it." It is the energy that flows from direct effort and the conversion of potential energy into kinetic energy or physical activity. This field is observable, quantifiable and measurable. It follows closely the laws of cause and effect.

Activities tend to be described and executed in a linear, serial fashion with one activity following another. The time dimension associated with this field is close to immediate. When we take action, we see the results immediately.

Since the results are close in time to our action, the corrective feedback loop is also almost immediate. For example, when you place a document in the copier and push start, you get immediate feedback about the desired results. You will either get the desired copy or you will have to make an adjustment such as remove a paper jam.

A more complex example is a factory line. In a canning factory, for example, a packing machine loads all the cans onto a conveyor that boxes them for shipping. If a can gets stuck, the belt backs up and cans eventually fall to the floor.

Observing this situation, an employee can, in a timely manner, stop the line, remove the stuck can and make sure everything is boxed accordingly. If you want to box more, you speed up the line or add more belts. The relationship to what we do and the results we produce is directly observable and measurable.

Some activities, such as creating a graphic design for someone else's approval, have a longer response time. Yet the feedback loop, the time between action and result, is still close enough to allow for timely adjustments until the desired outcome is accomplished.

The nature of information contained within the Activity field is linear and sequenced in a straight cause and effect orientation. Accordingly, the skills we need to receive, process and interpret this field's information are analytical or left brain skills. We usually measure a person's ability to succeed in these types of endeavors with such metrics as cognitive and spatial intelligence or simple IQ tests.

Relationship - the Energy of Interactions

Relationship

* Who We Do It With (Interactions)
* Communication
* Empathic
* Patterns
* Right Brain
* Emotional Intelligence

If Activity is the energy of what we do, Relationship is the energy of whom we do it with, the energy of our interactions. The Relationship field contains the energy that emanates from one person interacting with the energy fields of other people.

The dominant form of energy exchange in this field of energy is communication. It includes both what we say and how we say it. It appears to our brain as both a verbal and non-verbal exchange. In the verbal aspect, the energy is observable and processed through our senses, mostly our sense of hearing. In its non-verbal form, it is not so easily identifiable and observable. Yet the exchange of energy is still very real and present. We simply process the non-verbal energy through means other than our five senses. This information carries more weight in our decisions than the information processed through our senses. We discussed this in the section on intuition and "gut feelings."

Think about listening to a song. In every song, there are the lyrics and music. The lyrics are the verbal communication, the energy of what we hear that is processed by the language processing center in our brain. The music, however, is not processed the same way. Most people experience it through a feeling state, not the sense of touch but rather something felt within the body, as if the vibration and rhythm of the music resonates with and causes our bodies to vibrate at the same frequency. We process non-verbal communication like this as something we feel in our bodies.

As another example, think about a time when someone said something to you that, though you heard the words, the meaning you experienced was quite different. A common situation is when someone is feeling upset, you ask them about it and they snap back, "I'm alright, nothing's wrong." While you hear the words, you do not accept them as true. In fact, you give preference to what you experience from the non-verbal exchange of energy over the verbal exchange. If the words contained within the message are in alignment with the music of the message, then we experience the communication as authentic and trustworthy. If they are not in tune with our expectations and experience, however, we will always believe the non-verbal feeling state over the overt meaning of the message.

Non-verbal communication occurs in all areas of business. In one on one communication with your customers, employees, and suppliers as well as in group settings, what you say and the non-verbal energy that carries the music of your message determines whether the message is received as authentic or dismissed as so much hype. Simply put, it is not lyrics but the music that defines the message received.

The Relationship field is not time based. The energy flow is non-linear in nature and does not follow discernable, cause-effect patterns. Because it is non-linear, we must draw upon a different set of skills to process and interpret this information. Instead of the left-brain, analytical skills so prized in our current business models, Relationship energy is processed by the right brain. Relationship energy requires our ability to discern patterns of behavior, their underlying motivations, and experience empathy. We are fortunate that over the last few decades the work of emotional intelligence experts helped define the skills and characteristics required to process information from this type of energy.

Perhaps the most well known within the business community is the work of Daniel Goleman. In 1995 he published the book, *Emotional Intelligence*[15]. Goleman identified four specific skill domains: 1) the ability to recognize and understand your own emotions, 2) the ability to manage your emotions, 3) the ability to recognize and understand the emotions of others, and 4) the ability to manage the emotions of others. Collectively these four skills give us insight into and a map to improve a person's ability to work with their emotions and those of others. It is what determines one's ability to work with the energy of the Relationship field. And as many have come to accept, success is often governed more by a person's EQ than their IQ. EQ assessments have become a standard part of most organizations' assessment and coaching toolboxes.

Relationship energy adds to the energy of effort, the energy of the Activity field flowing through the organization. It has the ability to multiply the sum of all the individual energy contributions.

CHAPTER 7

> *"Coming together is a beginning; keeping together is progress; working together is success."* **Henry Ford**

Synergy - Multiplier Effect

We have all heard the term synergy. It is often euphemistically defined as two plus two equals five. This means we are experiencing the dynamic increase of the energy in the Relationship field when two people are attuned to the same energy frequency and the whole suddenly becomes greater than the sum of the individual parts. As we all know from our own observations and experiences, synergy is a powerful phenomenon. It has a huge multiplier effect on the amount of energy contributed by the collective in direct proportion to their level of attunement. Unfortunately, it was not easy to create it in our old model of thinking.

In our current model, we use the concepts of teamwork and collaboration to spark synergistic energy within our organization. To accomplish this, we stimulate better teamwork by changing processes, which is an Activity field effort. Examples of these efforts are the implantation of new tools such as Knowledge Systems, or through changes in workflow to facilitate cross-functional team interactions. Both are designed to stimulate better teamwork by changing processes. Both however ignore the underlying nature of Relationship energy. In our current thinking, we believe that Activity drives Relationships, when in fact it is often the other way around.

An Orange County, California internet infrastructure client was struggling with their lead conversion rate. They had developed a robust marketing campaign to create greater awareness of the new offerings and to generate additional leads, which they were getting. Yet the sales organization was complaining that the quality of the leads they were getting were poor and there was no mechanism to screen out the serious leads from the "lookie-loos." We helped create a new process for screening the leads which included defining a set of criteria that determined a qualified lead and integrated the communication of leads and lead follow up with their Customer Relationship Management (CRM) system. We also implemented a lead administration function to manage the lead conversion and follow up process. As we tracked the expected progress of this new set of processes, we found that after three months there was no change in lead conversion rates. In fact, things were getting worse. The sales force continued to complain that the leads were of no value and now marketing was arguing that sales couldn't close if they provided a lead that was ready to buy.

The problem was clearly not a process issue. It was a relationship issue. The VP of Sales did not believe in the marketing department's ability to attract good leads and had little respect for the VP of Marketing. The VP of Marketing felt the VP of Sales was a terrible manager and couldn't organize a two-house paper route, let alone lead an international sales organization. The beliefs each of the VPs held about each other trickled down to their organizations. With the chaos spinning in the Relationship field, no change in process or Activity energy would produce positive results.

Once we cleaned up the relationship issues between these two vice presidents and their departments, the lead generation process we put in place increased their lead conversion rate by 57% and improved sales by 32%.

In most companies the Relationship issues are never addressed, rather they try to make adjustments to the various processes or the metrics to resolve these issues. When tool and process changes don't work in the Activity field, many leaders revert to the fallback position of using the carrot and stick form of motivation. They begin to play with various forms of incentive programs with the hope that this will resolve the Relationship issues.

The problem with this approach is that it is founded on the false notion that external incentives drive behavior. This is only partially true. Since incentives are based on metrics and metrics are part of the Activity field, incentives can only work on activity field issues. In a corollary to the age old phrase "you cannot legislate morality," you cannot incentivize relationships. When incentives are used to motivate behavior when Relationship needs are not aligned, they are experienced as a form of coercion. This can lead to an endless expenditure of Activity Energy (and money) that will never deliver the desired results.

Why don't incentives work? It's like using a hammer to strike a deal or forge an agreement rather than finding a way to tune into another's frequency and become simpatico with the other person's inner thoughts and feelings. Without aligning the energies of the Relationship field, you not only lose the multiplier effect of synergy, you also consistently lose energy through the system as conflict rides under the surface and causes added turbulence to the flow.

Another approach that is often employed to resolve Relationship turbulence is to simply tell those in Relationship chaos to get over it and get the job done. Sometimes this works but not very often. What you might get is a brief reprieve from the conflict, but it only goes underground to resurface at a later time, and usually with more force or with a never-ending round of low level sniping among the team. Either way the energy flowing through the system is severely limited and the speed of execution is significantly impacted.

Does this seem too "touchy feely" for you and your organization? Are you convinced all that matters is the numbers and the rest will take care of itself? Do you think it is a waste of time and money to open yourself and the living organism that surrounds you to such flows of empathic energy? Then consider your own experience with being part of a high performing team.

Can you remember how it felt when everyone worked in harmony, where conflicts among members didn't exist, and everyone was focused on the same goal? Remember how energized you were, how effortless the team seemed to produce the desired outcome. It was as if something magical was happening and the results you produced seemed to be far above what anyone would have imagined.

What would it be like to have a whole organization operating like this? Impossible you say. I think not. It is difficult, even challenging. But if it can be achieved by single group, it can be achieved by every group. All we need is the right model that allows us to replicate it. Does this mean you have to become a touchy-feely leader? Perhaps it is time to put aside any past prejudices and experience the world around you in ways you never thought possible. Opening to such possibilities will produce results that go beyond what you thought was possible for your organization. It will move your organization to produce magical results like Apple, Whole Foods or Trader Joes.

Synergy Explained

No earlier model of management could explain the phenomenon we call "synergy." Our new model, with its deeper understanding of hidden energy fields, solves this problem.

By understanding communications, verbal and non-verbal, as waves of energy, then as we learned from physics, when two waves are in synch their energies are amplified. When the waves are out of synch, they are attenuated or diminished. It is really that simple. When two people interact, their interactions will be either amplifying their energy or attenuating it.

When people's energies are in synch, this is referred to as being in tune with each other or attunement. When two or more people are attuned, we experience the magic of synergy. On the other hand, when people are out of synch, their energies are attenuated. One of the interactions that create people being out of synch is misunderstood communication.

Misunderstandings take on many forms and have a number of root causes. One might be as simple as miscommunication. I said one thing and you assumed I meant something else. Or I used a certain word that had a specific meaning to me and you heard what I said but not what I meant. Interestingly enough, this happens to me quite often because of my Brooklyn accent. I say "water" and many people hear it more like "worda." It creates some humorous times at home as my wife, who is from Minnesota, tries to figure out just what the heck I'm saying and whether or not we're even speaking the same language!

Misunderstandings can also assume deeper, more complex forms. For example, the listener can clearly and correctly hear what is said but the meaning received is nothing like the meaning intended by the person communicating.

I was approached by the CEO of an Internet Marketing company in California. The CEO was concerned by the degree of bickering among the executive team. While some amount of conflict was OK the CEO was concerned that it reached a point of significantly impairing the organization's results. From the very first round of interviews it was very clear that this was more than simple bickering, this was a misaligned team. This group of executives was not on the same page about anything. The major conflict originally showed itself as differences between the Engineering department and the Sales organization, mostly around the prioritization of the product development roadmap. At first I thought the issue would be resolved by a simple implementation of a product prioritization process but it quickly became clear that the issue ran deeper than that. The CTO seemed to think that the core purpose of the company was to develop a robust technology platform that would enable a range of offerings to the SMB (Small and Medium size Business) market. The Sales Manager, and most of the rest of the organization, felt the core purpose of the company was to provide marketing services to the SMB market. The difference is subtle but it goes to the very core of what the company was about and how it would allocate resources to achieve its core mission.

How could such a rift exist? The CEO, explaining the mission of the company, said it was to provide marketing services for the SMB market and that their competitive advantage was their unique technology platform that allowed them to scale the services with lower costs than the competition.

A simple misunderstanding? Perhaps. It is easy to see how each side could interpret the CEOs comments to support their preferred position. The CEO, like so many other CEOs, thought that by creating common goals (Activity field) the team will naturally pull together. It did not. Without clearing out this misunderstanding, the Relationship field went into chaos. This rift, this simple misunderstanding prevented the organization from being able to execute on anything. It polarized the organization into camps and nearly brought it down.

In The Living Organization® model, misunderstandings are forms of energy loss from within the Relationship field. This energy loss can easily become multi-tiered. The first level of loss we experience is in the simple act of expending energy to clarify and correct misunderstandings. A second level of energy loss will arise in terms of feelings towards the other person, often feelings of hurt, anger, distrust or some other negative or protective emotion. This directs energy away from our focus on creating desired results and aims it towards protecting ourselves from hurt, expressing our anger or frustration with the situation, or simply feeling drained by it all. Remember how draining it can be to leave a meeting where people are bickering over what seemed like petty details and nothing got done? Clearly energy directed to Relationship turbulence is energy not directed towards the desired outcomes.

In addition to losing energy in the Relationship field we also will lose energy from the Activity field due to Relationship field turbulence. We lose Activity energy when we redirect it from the creation of results to actions required to correct the patterns of distrust. There is also the loss of Activity energy because of the rework effort required to fix the mistakes that happened because of the original misunderstanding. Misunderstandings can produce what we engineers refer to as "a cascading event" resulting in a colossal failure on our part to conserve energy and direct it towards the desired outcomes.

Turning the energy loss from a situation into a systemic loss of energy can further compound the problem. When we have a misunderstanding that is associated with a person of authority, the feelings we acquire about that leader are transferred to the organization as a whole. This takes the form of organizational distrust that negatively affects all our future interactions with everyone in that organization.

Communication misunderstandings at the organization level have a doubly disastrous impact on the total energy flow throughout the system since *much more energy must be expended to correct the situation*.

We can understand the impact of blocked communication flows to our organization by drawing an analogy to the how the human body functions. Think of the damage to the human body when you block the flow of energy between interacting organs. Parts of the body no longer function as intended. Any blockage of energy shuts down vital systems and forces the body to re-route the necessary flow of blood or energy, using up precious reserves in the process of restoring order to the body. Similarly, what starts off as a simple miscommunication can turn into major traumas to your Living Organization®.

The good news is we can reverse the situation and go from misunderstanding to attunement. Attunement is when the energy, Relationship and Activity, flows effortlessly among all parts of the organization, connecting and supporting each other. We have within us the necessary mechanism and almost all of us have used it at one time or another, though we may not have consciously known what we were doing.

Most people have experienced a situation where they are so attuned to another that they can almost anticipate what the other is going to do. We see this in married couples where one person can finish the sentences of another or in-tune teammates where one player moves to where the ball or puck suddenly is passed without a word passing between them. The famous hockey player Wayne Gretsky was known for his ability to know where the puck would be and somehow get there right before it arrived. "Skate to where the puck will be, not where it is," was how he would explain it. In business, we see this when one member of the team can anticipate the needs of the other team members. Ask them how they knew "where the puck will be," so they could have what was needed ready without being asked and they will likely answer, "I just knew."

In 1996, I joined a technology incubator as the President and General Manager of one of their portfolio companies. I joined the firm at the same time as Dave who headed up one of the other portfolio companies. About six months into my tenure, I was visiting our research facility at the University of British Columbia in Vancouver, Canada with Fred, the Founder and CEO of the incubator. During dinner Fred reflected on the difference between me and Dave.

"I don't understand it," he said.

"Understand what," I asked?

"When I hired you and Dave, I was sure Dave would turn out the better of the two. During the interview process you came across as a man who knew his own points of view and I thought you would be difficult to manage. Dave on the other hand was very clear that he understood he was the Captain and I was the General. His role was to understand my objectives and carry them out. Yet after just a short six months it seems the reverse has happened. Dave leaves me nothing but nightmares. I tell him what to do and he seems to do the opposite. It's as if he doesn't really understand what I expect of him. You on the other hand seem to know exactly what I expect. You have an uncanny ability to anticipate my every move. You know when to bring an issue to my attention and when you should just handle it. And it doesn't seem to follow any pattern. You will bring me a $200 issue and handle a $200,000 dollar issue on your own. And the amazing thing is you are always right. It's as if you are inside my head and know my every thought. How do you do it?"

How did I do it? A simple answer is that for the first three months I would watch and observe. I would ask Fred to explain why he was doing what he was doing so I could discern the pattern of his thinking. I could begin to see what was important to him and what wasn't. This is the beginning of achieving the state of attunement and it goes deeper. It goes to the ability to allow my Relationship field to resonate with his, which would allow me to pick up the energy pattern of his thinking.

It is clear from both these examples that some other form of communication is occurring through a much richer and more effective channel than mere verbal communication could explain. Heretofore this could only be viewed as a mysterious force at work, but by recognizing it as the transfer of energy, specifically Relationship energy, we can learn to create it and utilize it to our advantage.

In the example above, with this level of attunement between the two of us, we could operate much faster and much more effectively. The flow of energy between us was such that we would energize each other. This exchange of energy between us not only made us more effective, we found that it also increased the energy flowing through the entire system. Imagine what would happen to your Living Organization® if you could create the same impact? How would that increase the effectiveness and the value of your organization?

CHAPTER 8

> *"It takes 20 years to build a reputation and five minutes to ruin it. If you think about that, you'll do things differently."* **Warren Buffett**

Experience: The Driver of Perceived Value

As mentioned earlier, a company's revenue is a function of the marketplace's perceived value of its goods and services. And a component of that perception is the experience they have with the products, the people and the organization as a whole. It is the energy of *experience*, another critical element of Relationship energy, which has the largest impact on perceived value.

This is more than just your customer or client's interaction with your organization, though those interactions do have a significant impact on the experience itself. The experience I'm talking about is the energy that is actually felt by a customer. This energy takes the form of emotional and psychic responses that gets burned into their brain as your "brand experience." It's what they remember most about your product or service and the emotional reason they seek it out or avoid it like the plague.

Experience is the energy that lies underneath the activities of interaction with your people, processes, and products. It provides them with an unseen but quite real jolt of energy that either repels or attracts them to you. We can see this in a simple example of buying and enjoying a cup of coffee.

When you want to buy a cup of coffee, you have many choices, which can be simplified into two general categories. The first group includes stores that offer other products along with the coffee like donut shops, bagel shops, or convenience stores like 7-Eleven or AM-PM. It might even be your neighborhood McDonalds. The second category would be the dedicated coffee establishments like Starbucks, Peets Coffee, and the many single store locations that focus on the coffee experience.

With both categories, you can get the same basic product, whether a decaf mocha latte or a simple cup of black coffee. My wife and I often frequent our local Chevron Miles on the Run Mini-Mart and make a 24 oz cup of decaf coffee with chocolate syrup and steamed milk. What a Starbucks "Venti decaf mocha with 2 pumps and no whip" for $4.75 costs just $1.39 at our local Chevron station. Why would we pay over $3.35 more at Starbucks than at the local convenience store? The product, coffee, varies little between the two locations. In fact, the value of the coffee as a product, the commodity price, is $1.39. Why, then, is Starbucks able to charge a higher premium for what is essentially the same product? It is the "Starbucks Experience." There is something seductive in what Starbucks has created that keeps customers coming back for more. The difference is in the feeling, the experience of being there.

The difficulty in understanding the nature of experience is that it is not what a person or organization does that creates it, it is who they are being as they are doing it. Yes, there is personal service when you walk into Starbucks and order your coffee, but there is also an energy that emanates from the baristas that serve you. They may say, "Good morning Norman, your usual Venti decaf mocha this morning?" and it is the energy they say it with that will create the experience. If they are truly glad to see me, I will experience their caring. If they have learned to read a script and their voice is bereft of any true feelings, I will experience that I am dealing with a robotic machine and have a very different experience.

This creates the Starbucks Experience. When in Starbucks or similar establishments, you receive much more than a cup of coffee. You are buying the experience that Starbucks offers. The experience has the additional value of $3.35.

Most of us make our buying choices based on criteria other than the just the product we are buying and often are willing to pay more for that something extra. The Apple experience makes products with average technical functionality stand out by creating an experience that is more than the product design or the user interface. It is their whole experience universe, from the buying experience to the support after sale and their uncanny ability to reframe the business model for delivery of content.

What about Nordstrom, which set a new standard for the shopping experience that transcended just the act of buying clothes? Or the experience of shopping at Trader Joe's where people experience the attentive customer service, limited yet quality choices and a sense of adventure. Or the way the Whole Foods mission of making the world a healthier place is embraced by its employees, its suppliers, and its customers, creating an experience of belonging to something more than just shopping for groceries? Yes, products are important and so is price, but not nearly as impactful as the experience the customers have.

The fact is, *the experience of the brand* plays a critical role in most people's buying decisions. We said brand experience, not branding or brand image. Image can be manufactured and promoted. Experience of the brand is the energy that is associated with the brand, the energy felt by the customer. It is Relationship field energy, pure and simple. Image and the act of branding is a form of Activity Field energy that is attuned to the logical, rational mind. It is not what you say or do that counts. It is the energy you project in what you say or do that creates the experience that is felt. Experience is an emotional feeling that cannot be manufactured. What is felt is the authentic nature of the organization. It is a separate source of energy, which The Living Organization® can capture and cultivate through conscious choices.

Years ago my wife had confronted me about my feelings towards something she had done. I don't recall the specifics of the issue but what I remember so clearly was how I tried to convince her that it wasn't true. While all the words and arguments I had so carefully constructed should have convinced her that what she was experiencing wasn't accurate, it didn't work. I even tried hard to convince myself it was true. In the end what I realized was she was picking up on my true, authentic feelings, even if I wasn't willing to acknowledge it, either to her or even to myself. When I was willing to admit that what she was sensing was accurate we could then resolve the real issues.

It is like our earlier example of a song with its interwoven music and lyrics. The lyrics are what we say or do, but the energy of the music carries the truth of our authentic feelings. The same is true for your organization. You can spin your message any way you want; however, what the customers will experience is your authentic being. This is the power of the Relationship energy. It is a separate source of energy that The Living Organization® can capture and cultivate through conscious choices.

Perception produces margin

In every Living Organization®, your cells (people) and organs (sales, marketing, manufacturing, etc.) interact with Living Customers and other Living Entities in the marketplace. Whether it is during the sales process or the initial contact with a receptionist, there is an interaction and an exchange of energy. Similar to the discussion on Synergy in the previous chapter, this interaction and exchange will either amplify the energy and create a positive experience or negate the energy, creating a negative experience. Where the Relationship field's Synergy energy adds to or subtracts from the contribution energy, the field's Experience energy adds to or subtracts from the perceived value the customers place on your goods and services. And perceived value, in the end, determines the revenue you receive.

In order to survive at such high densities, the cells created structured environments. These sophisticated communities subdivided the workload with more precision and effectiveness than the ever-changing organizational charts that are a fact of life in big corporations.[16]

In order to survive at such high densities, the cells created structured environments. These sophisticated communities subdivided the workload with more precision and effectiveness than the ever-changing organizational charts that are a fact of life in big corporations.[17]

As a simple formula this would be expressed as $R = PV = FV + EV$, where R is Revenue, PV is Perceived Value, FV is Functional Value and EV is the value associated with the experience. Returning to our previous example of buying coffee, the functional value would be the physical product of coffee itself. The experience value would be the amount of value the customer assigned to the quality of all the Relationship interactions. Starbucks gets an additional $3.35 per cup simply because of the experience value.

As shown in Figure 10, adding Experience as a mutual exchange of energy between the customer and the people of the organization expands the model and furthers our efforts to uncover and understand the path to creating the magical results we dream of.

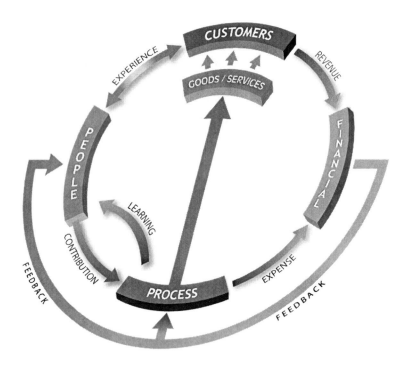

Figure 10

CHAPTER 9

> *Life is without meaning. You bring the meaning*
> *to it. The meaning of life is whatever you ascribe*
> *it to be. Being alive is the meaning.*
> **Joseph Campbell**

Where the Magic Hides

Context - the Energy of Meaning and Purpose

Context

* Meaning & Purpose
* Culture
* Holistic Knowing
* Connective
* Heart Brain
* Spiritual Intelligence (SQ)

This is the energy that flows from doing that which we desire - following our passion. It is the "why" of what we do, the field of meaning and purpose. This field of energy is mostly un-observable to scientists today. However, its presence is strongly felt. It is what influences and even determines what happens in the other two fields of energy: Activity and Relationship. Context makes its presence known through felt experiences, an energy we feel in our bodies such as the "team spirit" of a highly functioning sports team or the "esprit de corps" of the elite military organizations.

To further understand this sensory experience, think of walking into a room with a high degree of tension. Nothing needs to be said, nor does anything have to happen, yet the energy of tension can be felt: it is palpable. It is at this level of "felt sense" that Context energy travels through individuals and organizations.

Within organizations, the Context field is often incorrectly referred to as the culture of the organization. It is this but is also much more. Culture is part of Context but not all of it. Context is certainly much more than the "do's and don'ts" we associate with the word culture in our society. It's even more than the mores and shared values we spend so much time dissecting and diagramming.

It's the sum total of all our shared stories, the mythology we make up to explain our world to ourselves and to others. As such, it is not something that we can easily observe or measure but it literally defines "how we do things around here." An organization and the individuals within it cannot behave or operate in ways that are contrary to the Context framework defining the organization.

One can visualize the power of the Context field if one thinks of it as a container of water. The water takes the shape of the container, so in essence the container defines the shape of the water. Similarly the Context field serves to define the shape, the very nature of the organization. All behaviors that occur at the Activity field and the feelings of the Relationship field are likewise defined and limited by the Context field container.

Ever notice how an organization takes on the personality of its leader? I worked with a technology company whose founder and CEO had a strong tendency to avoid conflict. In fact whenever he had to deliver "unpleasant news" to someone, he usually had his VP of Human Resources do it. This set the Context field energy into a certain pattern and the culture of the organization as a collective operated with the same conflict avoidance attributes. People would rarely be direct with one another and the ability to effectively resolve differences and issues was seriously diminished. To change this pattern we had to redefine the stories that set the boundaries of this Context field container.

The Context Field contains energy associated with meaning and purpose. It is the energy that drives what is known in today's business environment as engagement. When people operate with only Activity Energy, their level of engagement is low; they are merely doing a job in exchange for a paycheck. When what they do taps into their own personal sense of meaning and purpose, they draw on a deeper pool of energy from their own personal Context field.

At a management workshop I attended I heard the story of The Three Bricklayers. A man walking down the street sees three bricklayers building a wall. Curious how these men view their rather back-breaking work, he approached each of them and asked, "What are you doing?" The first bricklayer answered, "What does it look like I am doing? I am laying bricks. I put the mortar down and then lay the brick. I do this every day, all day long." The second bricklayer answers, "I am laying bricks to build the wall of this building." The third bricklayer answers with a sense of excitement, "Why, I am laying bricks to help build this cathedral to the greater glory of god. It is such an honor to have such a wonderful job."

When you give people a sense that their activities have a deep sense of meaning and purpose, they will contribute a far greater amount of energy to their efforts and will "come alive." They become committed and passionate and fully engaged in what they do. For people who are committed and engaged by their passion, the act of doing actually gives them energy. This is why we commonly refer to such individuals as fully enlivened.

In an earlier chapter I referred to the energy that volunteers at non-profits have access to and asked what it would be like if this energy was available to your company? When I first joined HP in 1973 I joined the Neely Sales Region as a Systems Engineer. I was with the company about six months and I could already feel there was something unique about this company that drew people to want to do more than just what was expected, an attitude and energy that was in stark contrast to my previous four years at Pratt & Whitney.

I remember attending my first region sales conference. I sat through the regular meetings, presentations of new products, reviews of results, and projections for the following year. I also remember a little sales motivation game the Region Sales Manager had us partake in. He wanted to stress the importance of keeping in contact with our customers. Of course this was long before cell phones and pay phones were a common tool for the road warrior. He had everyone come up and dip their hand in a bucket of dimes and whatever you could take out you could keep.

Why did this simple exercise remain with me for all these years? For one, I was not a salesperson. For another, I was brand new to the organization. Yet, I was part of this team, a fully accepted member. And

Neely wasn't just any sales team, our region was the best of the best and I was accepted into that elite club, not because of anything I did to prove myself but simply because I was part of the team. This simple act created a sense of pride, a sense of belonging, and a desire to contribute above and beyond. There was no way I was going to let my team down.

Was it the simple game of grabbing a handful of dimes? Was it the fact that I was accepted? Was it that special feeling I experienced just being part of this organization, the sense of pride, the desire to serve customers that seemed to be everywhere? Perhaps it was all of that and more. I do know that the energy I gave during my tenure at HP was far greater than at Pratt & Whitney. I was not the only one who was that committed and passionate about what we did at HP. Not everyone was that engaged, but there were a lot more engaged employees passionate about success than not, a condition that is often the opposite in many companies.

The Soul of the Organization

My sense of engagement came from a sense of feeling that what I did made a difference. I felt that HP was an organization where I could more fully express what was important to me. I was able to tap into and express my deeper sense of meaning and purpose.

So far we have been describing the organization as flows of energy. One can correlate this to the physics or biology of a Living Organization®, the nature of the different forms of energy and how they flow throughout the organization. Drawing on the parallel between the corporate body and the human body, we know that the human body can likewise be described in terms of its physics and biology, or physiology. But we also know that there is more to being human than merely our physiology. Similarly, there is more to an organization than its physiology or physical makeup.

The hidden flow of thoughts, beliefs, and passions are part of the subtext of living systems, whether individuals or your company. It stands to reason that, like people who have a deep purpose and reason for doing what they do, your company also carries within it the energy of its deeper purpose, the very thing that animates it. The Context field is where this most critical source of energy resides – its Soulful Purpose™ as show in Figure 11 on the next page.

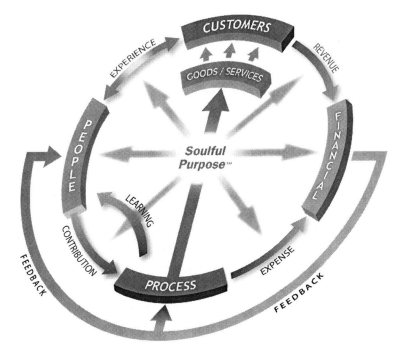

The Living Organization®
Figure 11

Your Company is a Living System that Directs the Flows of Energy, Transforming them into Desired Results, Fulfilling Its Soulful Purpose™.

All living things come into being for specific and important reasons defined by this deeper purpose. I don't believe it is pure randomness that brings such a variety of energy patterns together to form a particular living entity, whether it is a cell, a human being or a company.

I believe that energies flow into specific patterns we call life forms for a very specific reason, a reason that somehow serves Life itself. Whether this purpose is programmed into us by what some will call God, the forces of DNA, or the natural flow of an evolutionary impulse, I leave to others to ponder. What I do know is that an acorn is born to become an oak, a liver cell serves its Soulful Purpose™ best by becoming part of the liver, heart cells become part of a heart, and heart and liver become part of the body. Each living entity takes on a specific pattern of energy that allows it to effectively serve some purpose, giving that living entity a unique reason for existing.

Often to accomplish this purpose a single entity draws together with other similar "like minded" entities to form a collective that enables it to better realize its purpose. Atoms form molecules, a collection of molecules come together to form cells, cells form organs and collectively they form the human body. People come together to form teams, teams come together to form departments, and departments come together to form your company. Each comes together based on a shared desire to serve a common purpose and achieve a common result by pooling their genes, efforts and energy together to transform that collective force into collectively desired results.

The desired result we seek to accomplish emanates from the living entity's Soulful Purpose™. It is that Soulful Purpose™ that defines every entity's reason for being.

It is also an attracting and aligning force. I am attracted to become part of an organization, a collective of other living entities, because of a deep-felt sense, conscious or not, that this group will add to my ability to achieve my personal Soulful Purpose™. To the degree my Soulful Purpose™ is aligned with the Soulful Purpose™ of the organization I am with, my actions will further the purpose of the organization as it in turn furthers my purpose for being.

The Soulful Purpose™ is the core reason for our being and permeates all other activities and relationships. It is our unique way of being in service to the world and leaving behind a lasting legacy. It defines and determines the contribution we are destined to make and how we will make it. In the human form of energy, the Soulful Purpose™ helps define from the beginning of our life whether we should become an engineer or an artist, a dancer or a painter. In its business form, the organization's Soulful Purpose™ defines what role that particular company will play on the stage of business, the unique contribution it will make to our community as a whole and the market that company can best serve. The Soulful Purpose™ expresses itself in the Activity field in the form of the goods and services it provides to the customers it serves and in the Relationship field in the people who are drawn to work for that company or buy its products.

Access the Wisdom

Whereas Activity is linear in nature and Relationship is oriented around patterns, the Context Field is holistic in nature. It is not something that can easily be dissected or examined in pieces. Context most commonly manifests itself in what may be called "the totality of experience." It is also the source of intuition, insights and wisdom.

It is the one field of energy that connects us to all other fields and their associated patterns of energy. The illustration in Figure 12 will provide a useful metaphor to help understand the nature of this connective characteristic of the Context field.

While the iceberg is seen as a separate entity floating within the ocean, we also know that the Iceberg comes from the ocean and is made of the same material as the ocean, water. It is the ocean only in a different form.

Figure 12

Like the iceberg we also are immersed in a field of energy that is the same material only a different form. This field of energy has many names sometimes referred to as life energy, chi, or our inner spiritual field of energy. But I think of it simply as the infinite field from which everything emanates.

Like the currents within the ocean that move the icebergs around there is a flow to the energy of the Context field. I believe this flow directs life towards evolution, towards expansion and growth.

There is a flow of energy that guides life to evolve to ever-higher life forms, towards merging into more complex forms with increasing levels of awareness and consciousness.

The waves of energy emanating from the iceberg in the illustration are the waves of Relationship energy. It is the "communication" between one energy source and another. It is the lyrics and music being shared between two living entities. There is always information being transmitted between living entities. In our metaphor it is the energy between two icebergs as well as the iceberg and the collective field of the ocean.

That is not hard to visualize. Think of the communication you have with another. The information you are about to share is an expression of what you are experiencing, your personal Context. This could be an experience of joy or sadness or it could simply be an experience of some idea or concept you have. We can return once again to our song metaphor and understand the metaphor at a deeper level. We know that what you will express consists of the words and the music of your communication. The words are the obvious part. They are what you say. The music is the part of the message that carries the words across the medium, the Context field that lies between the two of you. You can see that what we often refer to as non-verbal communication is a lot more than simply body language. It carries the deeper energy of your Context field, the deeper sense of meaning and purpose.

I took a communication workshop where one of the exercises was to communicate a certain feeling to my partner. The feeling was whispered to me so my partner would have no idea what I was attempting to communicate. In addition I could only use the phrase "fish jump high and fly." The feelings I needed to communicate were first upset, then anger and finally love. I was amazed at how accurately my partner could pick up on the emotions I was communicating. It's as if the state of experience I was holding was what she was also experiencing. I learnt that though we depend so much on words it is never the words that carry the real message. And it also taught me that my inner state, whether peaceful, calm, agitated, loving or upset, is what is received in the communication regardless of the words I used. The good news is that I have control over my state of being.

It is the Context field energy that is the power of the music. It is the energy that is defined by the vibration frequency the state of being I am experiencing at the moment. And the more I can fully connect my awareness to this state of being and authentically project it, the more accurately it will be received. This is the real definition of authentic communications. The words and the music are aligned and consistent. What I am experiencing in the moment is what I authentically share.

We also know information is a form of energy. Ideas and thoughts are simply another form of energy. A lot of information lies within our Personal Context field but, unless we learn how to draw on it, it remains below the surface of the ocean in our unconscious. In addition to what lies within our Personal Context field, one can imagine the vast amounts of information that lay within the Universal Context Field. Since we are all swimming in the infinite Context field then it would follow that we all have access to the information, the wisdom that lies within it, if only we could learn to tap into it.

Because of its connective nature, Context provides us information and insight about our environment that we do not have access to through our normal information processing centers. The "gut feel" or "intuitive insight" we often experience in our organizational life is really information coming into our consciousness from the Context Field. This information is what we often refer to as wisdom, the ability to understand our world at deep levels, to see the interconnectedness of all things, and the implications of our actions.

What makes collecting information from this field of energy different from all others is that the information does not pass directly through our senses and is not originally processed by the right or left hemisphere of mental processing. Rather, it is sensed via our body. It manifests itself as "shivers up the spine" or "tingling in your toes" and you know you're onto something.

Research done by Michael Gershon, chairman of the Department of Anatomy and Cell Biology at New York–Presbyterian Hospital/Columbia University Medical Center,[18] reveals that our digestive system contains some 100 million neurons, more than either the spinal cord or the peripheral nervous system. Emery Mayer, professor of physiology, psychiatry and bio-behavioral sciences at the David Geffen School of Medicine at the University of California, Los Angeles (UCLA), has discovered that about 90 percent of the fibers in the primary visceral nerve, the vagus, carry information from the gut to the brain and not the other way around.[19]

The HeartMath Institute[20] explored the physiological mechanisms by which the heart, also a neurological processing center, communicates with the brain. This path of communication significantly influences our brains information processing. Some of the first modern psycho-physiological researchers to examine the conversations between the heart and brain were John and Beatrice Lacey. During 20 years of research in the 1960s and '70s, they observed that the heart communicates with the brain in ways that significantly affect how we perceive and react to the world.

Further research by Dr. J. Andrew Armour, one of the early pioneers in neurocardiology, introduced the concept of a functional "heart brain" in 1991. His work revealed that the heart has a complex intrinsic nervous system that is sufficiently sophisticated to qualify as a "little brain" in its own right. The heart's brain is an intricate network of several types of neurons, neurotransmitters, proteins, and support cells like those found in the brain proper. Its elaborate circuitry enables it to act independently of the cranial brain – to learn, remember, and even feel and sense[21].

Whereas Activity Energy is processed by the left-brain and Relationship Energy is processed by the right-brain, modern research indicates that the body-brain, the heart-brain and gut-brain process Context Energy.

In an article written by Dr. Otto Scharmer, a Senior Lecturer at MIT and founding chair of the Presencing Institute, he states:

"I have spent the past 15 years observing, facilitating and co-leading change projects in different sectors, systems and cultures. What strikes me most about these experiences is that the basic problem is the same. It is that leaders facing problems respond to them by pulling all of the usual triggers. But more of the same will not be good enough. Leaders and managers face issues that require them to slow down and even stop; and then they need to start paying attention, listening, reaching out, listening more, sensing what wants to happen and reflecting deeply and connecting to an inner source of knowing."[22]

I believe that there is a relationship between the three information-processing centers of our body. The body-brain picks up information from our surroundings – the "ocean" of the Context field. This information is oriented towards a holistic sense, an experience of all that is around us. The information is first processed by our Heart-brain as felt experiences and is then passed to our right-brain where patterns are discerned. Those patterns give form and meaning to our experiences. From there, the information is presented to our left-brain, where it is sorted, catalogued and filed away for future reference.

While further research would be needed to prove this hypothesis, it serves as a working framework that enables us to engage all the information processing centers of our bodies. The intent, of course, is to give us greater access to more resources, allowing us to make even better decisions.

What gets measured gets improved

As noted, we have learned how to assess our skills and abilities with Activity Energy. A wide variety of tests, including cognitive skills test, IQ tests, and motor coordination tests, help us determine our ability to use logic and spatial orientation, the key skills for working with activity field energy. Since the mid 90s, we have been introduced to the work of Daniel Goleman and other researchers in the field of Emotional Intelligence. Emotional Intelligence (EQ) assesses our ability to relate to others and ourselves. It is one measure of our skills with Relationship energy.

The next frontier is to expand our ability to assess one's skills with the use of Context energy. There are already a number of attempts to establish a tool that can assess our Spiritual Intelligence or SQ[23]. Companies such as Nokia, Unilever, McKinsey, Shell, Coca-Cola, Hewlett Packard, Merck Pharmaceuticals, Starbucks and the Co-operative Bank are increasingly using models for developing and measuring spiritual intelligence in corporate settings[24]. At Quantum Leaders, we have been utilizing the SQi Assessment from Deep Change[25] with quite remarkable results for organizations and their leaders in deepening their access to the Context field wisdom.

Explaining the Unexplainable

We know that much of what happens in business cannot be explained by our existing models, which are based on the machine paradigm. The machine paradigm views everything through the lens of the Activity Field, the field of what we do and how we do it. If it cannot be reduced to actions, tasks and metrics, then it must be that woo-woo soft stuff. While the soft side of business is acknowledged, it is also easily dismissed as not as important as what we do or improving how we do it.

For the last half century, business has recognized that the machine paradigm, which all of our current business models depend on, has had many limitations. We have attempted to integrate into that paradigm the ideas of psychologists to improve our overall success, but it never reached the impact it should have.

Since the middle of the twentieth century we have introduced the concepts of teams and collaboration, mission/vision/values, strategy alignment, servant leadership, leadership versus management, and many other advancements in management theory. These ideas have become part of the management lexicon, but that seems to be as far as it has gone in most companies. Rather than integrating and morphing the fundamental machine paradigm, it became simply ideas bolted on top of the machine. And the power of the existing system overshadowed any real change. Even the newest ideas of Corporate Social Responsibility, Conscious Capitalism and Shared Value,[26] are forced to explain their value using the machine paradigm framework. Even though there is a large amount of evidence that these new ideas truly make a difference, they struggle for wide scale adoption. This is because paradigms define and frame our behaviors and decisions: any ideas outside the existing paradigm have no ground for existence. These movements have to rely on anecdotal evidence or "do good for goods sake and it will pay off," as ways to stimulate adoption and changes within the organization.

But the path of adoption of any new idea is long and difficult. And adoption will only begin to happen when the existing paradigm can be expanded to include new knowledge. When we cannot explain the results we experience within our existing paradigm, it is basic human nature to relegate it to luck, magic, the invisible hand, the ether, or the gods. Or we dismiss it as the workings of the unconscious, something that is equally beyond our control.

But then someone will come along and create a new model that better explains what we are experiencing about how life works. With the aid of these new models, we begin to understand that it is not merely the ether, but the laws of quantum physics; it is not the wind gods, but the interaction of physical laws. The evolving theories of psychology and human behavior better reveal the forces of the unconscious and make them available to us. Because of these new models, we now have more control over our behaviors and we have expanded our awareness, understanding and wisdom.

The Living Organization® is a new model for understanding all the forces of business and commerce. Understanding the energy fields that are at play, whether visible or not, helps us to make better decisions and guide our organizations through turbulent waters churned up by the forces under the surface of the visible Activity Field; the forces of Relationship and Context.

What has heretofore been relegated to the unexplainable, the soft-side of business, is now revealed to be very much part of the hard side of business. The three energy fields interact with an interdependence that creates the results we desire.

All Results Start In the Context Field

Back to basics, everything is energy and energy cannot be created or destroyed. Therefore what we experience as the results in our lives is the outcome of a process of transforming energy. The Context Field, the field of infinite possibilities, is the source of all manifestation. It is within the Context field that the journey of manifestation begins; the process of moving from the unformed to the formed, from the field of infinite possibilities to the field of physical form.

Personal and collective context sets the boundary conditions of what is possible, of what physical formations of energy can manifest. The meaning and purpose we ascribe to life lies within the Context field, which defines the boundaries of our world. It defines the shape of the container of our life, the particular iceberg so to speak.

The first step in the formation process is the translation of meaning and purpose into our values and our beliefs, which form our individual and collective worldview, our paradigms. These in turn define the boundaries of what is possible and what is not possible. Therefore the boundaries we weave out of the Context field will quite literally define what we can achieve and what we cannot. It will either propel us forward or hold us back.

The Dance of Energy

The three fields are in a constant flowing dance of interactions. For example, we will ascribe meaning to what we observe in the physical world of Activity which will impact our personal Context field and our Context field will set the boundaries of what experiences will take form in the physical world.

Eventually what we create will be the result of the activities we do, but the activities we do are governed by the relationships we have and both the activity and the relationships are governed by the context we hold.

If we just look at what we do, our activity, it might look something like Figure 13.

Figure 13

But almost every activity we do involves interactions with others as in Figure 14 below. One can view our activities as being held within a circle of relationships. These relationships will either support our activities or hinder our efforts.

Figure 14

Just as activity is held within a circle of relationship, both relationship and activity is held within the container defined by the context field, as shown in Figure 15.

Figure 15

A client in the information security industry needed to improve its win ratio on competitive bids. This contract engineering organization had gone through the process of redoing the proposal process and even hired a proposal manager to oversee and mange each proposal through the process. This however did not improve their win ratio. It was not until we identified the hidden forces restraining their success were they able to improve their performance.

The specific issue was that their cultural context was rooted in a sole-source bidding environment. In this environment, the key to success was their ability to develop the most elegant technical solution to the customer's' problems. This became a source of pride for the engineers and became what the company was known for.

As they advanced, their environment changed and they found themselves in more and more competitive situations. They were not winning because culturally, the engineers could not bring themselves to do anything less than the most elegant technical solution. They could not propose a plan that required a tradeoff that would diminish the technical solution so the proposal could stay within the budget constraints of the customer. It violated their core belief about what the company stood for.

All the costs associated with the changes to the proposal process and the salary of the proposal manager was lost, as were millions of dollars in lost business opportunities. It was not because these process changes were wrong, but because they were implemented without making the necessary changes in the Context field to realign the framework that defines what is possible, thereby allowing the needed process changes at the Activity level to take hold. Once we had redefined the container of the Context field their win-ration went from zero to 60% in two years.

It's All a Story

The pattern of our individual and collective container, our boundary conditions, is defined quite literally by the stories we tell. We believe what we believe because of the stories we tell ourselves about how life works. Those beliefs define the results we can and cannot create.

One simple guideline to examine life and your own successes and challenges is to know that everything outside of yourself is a reflection of what is happening inside. I use this framework to examine my own life and it often helps me discover things I am not conscious of as I do business.

The year 2010 was financially challenging for me as it was for many. In March I concluded an engagement with a large client, which left a serious cash flow shortfall. No matter what I did and I did everything one would do to create new business, nothing was happening. I was unable to create the results I wanted.

Knowing that my outside world is a reflection of my inside world and that activities and results are reflective of the Context field, I started looking there. I began a process of uncovering and exploring the stories embedded deep within my own personal Context, the stories that define my boundaries of what is and is not possible. There were many that related to money, value and worth and they carried a similar theme, a distinct pattern: "I am so different in the way I see things and no one appreciates it."

Logically, I knew I was appreciated by my many clients and could prove that I had contributed much value to them. But deep within my unconscious there was a different story. I felt the value of my contributions were never really good enough. I knew I had a lot of insight and understanding, but I also had the story that others couldn't possibly understand me and couldn't appreciate what I contributed. My behaviors were unconsciously following my inner story. I would be tentative with my insights, even apologetic for my point of view perhaps being different. It was the inner story I held that was governing my behaviors and what prospective clients experienced. With this worldview, is it any wonder that prospective clients wouldn't be attracted to me?

At the beginning of 2011, I began to weave a new story. I began to shift the pattern of the old story and in doing so I shifted the pattern of energy that defined my boundaries. The process is not one of judging my story or even trying to change it by will and determination. That would be like trying to tame a wild horse by whipping it back into a corner. Rather it is a process of observing and acceptance. A process of becoming friends with my story, acknowledging what part of it is true and how it has served me to this point in my life. From this place of compassionate acceptance, the energy is freed from this particular story pattern, releasing it to form a new pattern, a new story.

I continue to be attentive to my inner stories, the ones that define my world and my results. I continue to work with the energy flowing within my Personal Context to reweave those stories to be consistent with what serves me best today. While there is a part of this process that is intellectual, an Activity field process, it mostly requires the skills of working with the Context field energy. Only by engaging the Context field can we change the boundaries of what is possible.

This is a personal story and we all have them. But the same is true for your organization. It also carries deep within the collective unconscious the stories that define the Context boundaries of what is possible and what is not. And the same process that has worked on the personal level also works for the organization. It is a process of first observing and accepting the collective stories. A process of acknowledging what part of it is true and how it has served the organization to this point in its life. From a place of compassionate acceptance, the energy will be released from the old patterns and allowed to form the new patterns that will better support what you want to create.

Once new stories redefine the boundaries of the Context field, there is often a lag time before the results show up in the Activity field. This is why change is often so difficult, for we are accustomed to the cause effect relationship of the Activity field. But that often doesn't apply to the changes in the Context field.

Because of this it often requires a degree of courage, the courage to follow your deeper calling and allow life to unfold in ways that are not always predictable or within our control. I regularly explore my deeper sense of purpose, my personal Soulful Purpose™ and I clearly hear that the path I am on is the path I am meant to travel. This path remains my guiding compass and without knowing what will unfold I am confident it will yield results. I already sense my inner state of being is fundamentally different, and it is showing up in my behaviors. I engage people with a greater degree of confidence. I share my perspectives and insights with a greater feeling that it really makes a difference. I have begun to have more conversation with new prospects interested in my work.

As a lover of roses, I accept that roses bloom when the rose bush is ready. I can prepare the soil, plant the bush, cultivate the roses, fertilize, weed and water them, but I cannot tell the rose bush to bloom next Tuesday at 3 PM. The same is true of life. I can weed, fertilize and water the stories of my Context field and the roses of my life will bloom when the roses bloom.

My client with the win ratio challenge changed its results by also weaving a new story about the meaning and purpose of its organization.

When changing our processes does not create the results we want, we must look at Relationship and Context field energy patterns.

The results we produce start with the stories that make up our organization's context boundaries. Reweaving the stories to produce the required relationships and activities will produce the results we want. Our next book will explore further the art of storytelling and the power of reweaving of the boundaries of the Context Field.

CHAPTER 10

*"You cannot continuously improve
interdependent systems and processes until you
progressively perfect interdependent,
interpersonal relationships."* **Stephen Covey**

The True Nature of Business

We can now more fully understand the true nature of business. It is more than a machine concerned with the efficient production of goods and services to be sold to consumers. It is more than a printing machine for making money. It is more than the simple organization of human effort in a beehive of activity.

It is a living entity, a multi-dimensional being brought into life to create and fulfill its Soulful Purpose™. It is a living creative being born to make a unique contribution to society.

Business in 3-D

For the last 150 years we have been following the Newtonian view of business as a machine; a view systematized by the work of Frederick Taylor and the many management theorists that have guided our thinking. This is a simple, one-dimensional view of how we create results, a view that directs our focus on the Activity field of process improvement, metrics and quantifiable goals.

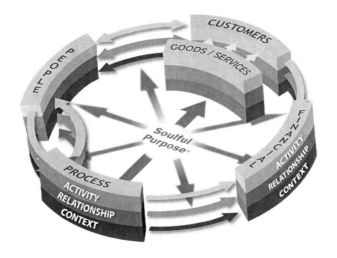

The Living Organization® in 3D
Figure 16

Earlier we described business and the act of creating results as a three dimensional dance of energy, as in Figure 16 above, of what we do and how we do it, who we do it with, and the underlying sense of purpose for why we do it: the Activity, Relationship and Context energy. It is the body, mind, emotion, and spirit of business, of The Living Organization®.

The rules of engagement change when we see our organization as living beings that are brought to life to create goods and services that bring value to those they serve. Rather than the limited view of life as a machine, we draw from the well of deeper wisdom of how life functions and we can apply the universal understanding of man's body and soul to our previous, inaccurate, model of the "cold, lifeless corporation."

In Figure 17 on the next page, we compare the attributes of The Living Organization® with those of "a machine of production."

Is it any wonder that organizations struggle to implement any real changes in business? When the Context field boundaries are set to that of the machine paradigm, no matter what we say or do, we will operate as if we are running a machine. We might truly believe people are our most important asset and we might say we are a learning organization, but the action at the Activity will stay in the boundaries of the machine paradigm.

The Living Organization	Machine
Creates	Produces
Organic Interdependent Relationships	System of Discreet Components
Learns and Adopts	Does What It Is Told
Purpose Is To Serve	Purpose Is To "Do"
Sense and Respond	Predict & Control
Relational	Transactional

Figure 17

When we take on the context of a Living Organization®, suddenly our organization springs to life. We move from life as a set of tasks to life as creation. We move from doing what we know we can do to doing that which creates the future we sense is possible and desire to create. We learn to cherish and nurture our organizations, to honor their purpose and marvel at their creation. We commit ourselves more completely and deeply to their survival, growth and lasting legacy.

We increase our ability to guide our organizations when we learn to work with the energies that flow throughout them and tap into the appropriate field for each challenge we face.

Creating results like those of Apple, Whole Foods and other Firms of Endearment companies does not have to be left to magic. This new science gives us the framework that allows us to release and guide the energy that creates the magic. We move from the one-dimensional space of the machine to the three-dimensional space of life and creation.

A Success Story

One of my professional service clients is a 50-year-old company that grew over the years through a combination of acquisitions and organic growth. For the first 45 years, its acquisition strategy followed standard rules. They evaluated what the target company did, looked at the financial benefits to the company to ensure it would be accretive, and made sure that the business processes were integrated post acquisition. They experienced the same average success rate of most companies when it comes to acquisitions. Some succeed. Most fail.

In 2001, the company began to transition from the founder to the next generation of management. By 2005, the company was under the leadership of the new CEO and his new executive team. They continued the strategy of growth through acquisitions with one exception; over the last six years they did seven acquisitions and all but one was successful. Six out of seven successful acquisitions. What was different?

While they still followed all the traditional activities of fit to strategy, accretive, and proper due diligence, they approached the process in a totally different way. In addition to the traditional Activity field issues, they focused on the Relationship field and the Context field.

They spend time understanding the Soulful Purpose™ of the target company, why it exists, what creates meaning for the employees and their customers. They understand the nature of the relationship the target has with all of its stakeholders, employees, suppliers, customers, and investors, not the nature of the transaction relationships but the nature of the relationship: the quality of the interactions it has with its stakeholders.

Under the new management, an acquisition is more like an adoption than a purchase. They are bringing a new member into their family and they want to make sure the new member gets as much out of the relationship as they will. They live within The Living Organization® model, not the machine of production model.

The Model Applied

In The Living Organization® model, the journey starts from the source, the people, and is transformed into the goods and services the organization provides its community, the customers it serves.

Figure 18

The people, individually and collectively, are the source and the conduit for the energy of the Context Field. They contribute this energy through efforts guided by the business processes, business models and infrastructure of the organization, all to serve their customers. Financial systems and other process metrics provide feedback on performance. People, process, and customers are, always have been, and always will be, three key domains of focus of every executive and CEO.

Another element that CEOs and executives focus on is – *Leadership*. While not explicitly called out in this model, we must recognize that leaders make up a distinct and important subset of the people. They perform the critical role of stimulating, directing and coordinating the flow of energy through the organization.

All the activities of a modern day corporation will fall into one of these four domains, shown in Figure 18 above.

The fifth element, **Financial**, is the measuring system. It is the gauge that allows us to determine the optimal balance between creating demand for our products and services and fulfilling that demand, represented by Revenue and Expenses.

Revenue is the measure by which the market values the goods and services we provide. It is the gauge measuring the demand from our customers and is associated with Customers and Products. Expenses are a function of efficient and effective use of energy flowing through the system and are therefore metrics associated with People and Process.

The ultimate determinant of an organization's success is how well these four domains – Leadership, People, Process and Customers - are optimized and in balance with each other.

Our current paradigm, as I have stated throughout this book, is outmoded in its ability to achieve this optimization and balance. All we can see through the lens of our current paradigm is Activity related energy. When a problem exists within our organization, the solutions we tend to implement will typically be within the Activity Field alone.

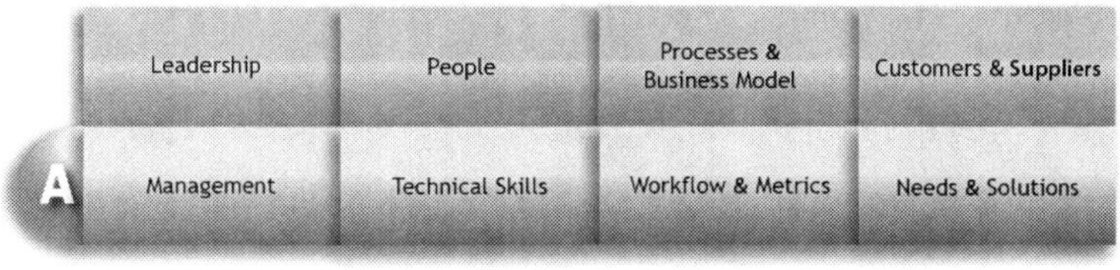

| Leadership | People | Processes & Business Model | Customers & Suppliers |
| Management | Technical Skills | Workflow & Metrics | Needs & Solutions |

Figure 19

While Activity energy and the changes we make to affect it are an important part of any solution, we must tap into the other two fields to achieve results. To open the lens wider and view a broader, more effective range of solutions, we must take into account how Relationship and Context energies play into our current challenges and what they might offer to provide a more complete and effective solution.

Let's expand our view of these four domains of The Living Organization® by looking at the kinds of issues each Energy Field addresses within the four key domains of business: Leadership, People, Process and Markets.

Activity

Figure 19 above shows the activity characteristics of each of the four domains. In the domain of Leadership, Activity energy defines the traditional role of management. This includes the functions of setting goals and targets, planning what needs to be done and organizing the work to get it done. It also includes the function of controlling the work, which includes establishing the metrics that define success and guiding the people's behavior in the organization. This is the activity of making sure that what needs to happen is happening.

Activity energy is the actual efforts of the people within the organization. It is where all potential energy is converted into kinetic energy, where the contribution energy is manifest. To be effective in the conversion of potential energy into kinetic energy and to maximize the contribution made by all, it is important to develop and improve functional and technical skills of the individuals and the collective organization. This is what determines how efficiently energy is converted into performing the tasks necessary to create the results.

Process is where we define the way the energy will flow throughout the system. It is where we define the tasks that need to be done and the order in which they should be accomplished. The goal of each Process is to make the flow of energy as frictionless as possible so there is minimum energy loss as the energy travels along its path to be transformed into goods and services. It is where we determine and define the underlying business model for the organization as a whole and the metrics that provide appropriate feedback for the amount of energy flowing through our organization, allowing us to monitor and improve our process. Over the years we have spent a lot of time and developed a number of methods and tools to help in the streamlining of business processes. Business Process Reengineering, Total Quality Management's Continuous Process Improvement efforts, Lean Manufacturing and Six Sigma are some of those tools.

The customer domain is where the actual Activity of exchange between the company and the customer takes place. It is where the parameters of success are determined. It is where we find out how well the organization understands and provides solutions to the needs of the customers they serve. This is where the organization decides what products and services to provide to serve specific communities. It is where the successful fulfillment of its goal can be measured, where value is transformed into revenue.

Relationship

The Relationship field, in Figure 20, adds another layer of complexity to the challenges and opportunities for creating the balance between demand and fulfillment, between revenue and expenses.

	Leadership	People	Processes & Business Model	Customers & Suppliers
A	Management	Technical Skills	Workflow & Metrics	Needs & Solutions
R	Teams & Collaboration	Interpersonal Skills	Orgainization Design & Information Flow	Brand & Reputation

Figure 20

The key attribute for leaders in the Relationship Field is their ability to build teams and foster collaboration among individuals and groups.

In the area of People, we are concerned with interpersonal skills and each individual's ability, as individuals and in collective groups, to communicate effectively, listen to, and empathize with others.

To define the flow of energy through any system, we have to take into account the interplay of energy flow from one component to another. We not only focus on the energy flow within the various functions of sales, marketing and operations, but we also pay attention to the way the energy flows between and around those units. For Relationship in the Process domain we are concerned with how the organization is designed to facilitate effective communication and information exchange between and among operational units.

The Relationship with the outside world focuses on our brand, our reputation, our relationships with our customers and our suppliers and all of the organization's constituencies. It even includes our relationship with our competitors, for they too play a key role in our failure or success.

Context

The Context field underlies all this as in Figure 21. It molds and guides what happens in the other two fields of energy. It defines what is and is not possible in the other two fields. It is one of the most critical fields of energy to learn how to work with because it is the structure that holds the other energy fields.

	Leadership	People	Processes & Business Model	Customers & Suppliers
A	Management	Technical Skills	Workflow & Metrics	Needs & Solutions
R	Teams & Collaboration	Interpersonal Skills	Orgainization Design & Information Flow	Brand & Reputation
C	Motivation & Inspiration	Intrapersonal Skills	Culture, Norms & Rules	Trend Dynamics

Figure 21

To stimulate the energy of the Context Field, leaders need the skill of inspiring and motivating others.

This is not a process of cajoling or manipulating but rather the ability to reach deep within others and engage what is meaningful to each. It is the ability to raise the level of passion, commitment and engagement in others that creates the additional energy available to The Living Organization® as a whole. This deeper sense of connection comes when what is meaningful to them is connected to what is meaningful to the organization. Their personal Context field energy is attuned to and stimulated by the flow of energy from the organization's Context field.

Leaders stimulate this connection by the stories they tell. Stories about why the organization exists, stories about the difference the organization makes, and stories about what is important around here all serve to set the boundary conditions of the Context field. You can determine what an organization's Context is by listening to the collective telling of their stories within the organization.

To maximize people's ability to contribute the greatest flow of energy requires developing their intrapersonal skills, as well as their interpersonal and functional skills. This enhances everyone's ability to gain a deeper understanding of their internal drivers: what motivates and sparks their passion. When individuals are capable of working for reasons other than mere survival, their level of energy contribution goes up exponentially.

This correlates with Maslow's Hierarchy of Needs in Figure 22 on the next page. Maslow's first level is physical and survival needs. This correlates to the Activity field, the work that needs to be done to ensure the organization can create and deliver its products and services, have enough resources and know it will survive and sustain itself.

The second level of Maslow's hierarchy addresses the social needs. This is supported by the Relationship field of the organization's interactions with its customers, it suppliers, and even its competition. It addresses the organization's need to know where it fits in the social order and its sense of connectedness.

The Context field relates to Maslow's higher order needs of Self-Actualization. It represents the organization's need to be and do that which it was "born to do," to fulfill its Soulful Purpose™.

The Context field is where we focus our building process to create the culture that moves and engages people. Culture is "the way we do things around here." It's reflective of the true, deeply held values of the organization, which may be very different from the espoused values we see hanging on the walls. This is the field from which the energy of the Soulful Purpose™ arises to infuse and give life to the whole living body of people we refer to as our corporation.

Communities of customers, like organizations, are also living entities we call markets. Like all living entities the dynamic forces of the Context field impact markets and the market's Soulful Purposes™ drive the trends and direction of market movements. The better organizations can understand these dynamic Context field forces, the better they will sense the markets' directions and be able to provide solutions ahead of their competition.

Figure 22

> *The only thing we know about the future is that it will be different. Trying to predict the future is like trying to drive down a country road at night with no lights while looking out the back window. The best way to predict the future is to create it.*
> **Peter Drucker**

Putting it all Together

Here we are again, our annual strategy retreat. As we begin to file into the room, each of us is filled with some excitement but mostly skepticism. How many of these have we been to? At first we thought this was a great idea but after the last five years, I think we have become somewhat jaded. They all seem to be the same. We start with a series of exercises to create some sense that we are all a cohesive team, followed by the sharing of a bunch of data, from which we are then led into a series of discussions to decide what our strategy should be.

Okay, the exercises are fun and we do learn something about our teammates. The review of the data does provide some useful insight and we do usually come up with some good ideas about what direction will give us the maximum results. Perhaps the best of these sessions is when the facilitator actually documents the results and produces a plan with specific initiatives with people responsible for them. But in the end, it always ends the same. We go back to our daily responsibilities and within the first quarter the plan is almost forgotten, that is until a year later when we get together to plan our strategy for the coming year. Then we realize how little we managed to get done since our last strategy session.

This vignette illustrates a common theme we experience with clients, independent of size or industry. In fact a number of studies show that 90% of strategies are never implemented. Strategy planning is a lot like New Year's resolutions – great ideas, poor implementation.

The problem is that companies put most of their focus on defining the right strategy and less attention to executing the strategy. Companies decide which strategy will provide the most competitive advantage given its unique strengths. They collect a lot of information about the market, the competition, and the needs of the customer. Then they decide which market positioning and branding to choose. They research the Voice of the Customer to understand what their needs are and what products would best satisfy them. They utilize strategy decision models such as SWOT analysis, Scenario Planning, and Delphi Analysis to anticipate the future. They use strategy-positioning tools such as Blue Ocean Strategy, Porter's Five Force Analysis, Environmental Scanning and War Gaming.

Missing in all of these methodologies is the need to execute the strategy. Yes, it is critical to define the most effective strategic direction, which when executed, will establish you as the leader in your industry. But to state the obvious, a mediocre plan well executed will outperform an outstanding plan poorly executed. We have seen over and over again very brilliant plans poorly executed. In fact only 10% of companies know how to execute well since 90% fail to execute on their stated objectives.

A New field – Strategy Execution

I once heard David Norton share a conversation he had with Renee Mauborgne, both giants in the field of strategy. David is co-author with Robert Kaplan of the world-renowned book *The Balanced Scorecard*; and Renee, with his co-author W. Chan Kim, wrote the international best seller *The Blue Ocean Strategy*. Renee asked David why *The Balanced Scorecard* is so much more popular, which took David by surprise.

"Renee," David responded, "how can you ask that when you have sold many more copies than we have?"

"Yes but wherever we go, *The Balanced Scorecard* is the most widely used system for strategy."

David thought a minute and then responded, "Renee, that is because you are swimming in a red ocean of defining strategy, while we are in the blue ocean of executing strategy."[27]

Strategy is often thought of as a noun; we have a strategy, here is our strategy, our plan. But strategy is really a verb, a set of actions to move the organization to a new way of being. Strategy is execution; it is a process of executing a set of initiatives that will get you to a desired outcome. Like the process of growth and development of individuals, growth and development of an organization is determined by the contribution–learning cycle we presented earlier in the book. Execution is synonymous with developing the organization. It is the process of taking actions designed to help the organization grow and develop to better serve the customers within its defined communities. It requires the holistic development of the organization to maximize the flow of all three fields of energy: Activity, Relationship and Context.

Execution Management is a process of managing the set of actions that will develop the organization's ability to perform and create its desired outcomes. As with many other processes such as project management, new product development and quality, execution management will be enhanced by a formal methodology. Without it, we are left to trust in the unique abilities of one or two leaders who have over time developed the intuitive ability to guide the organization through its execution process. This is like the early days of managing projects when successful project management required the skills of an "artisan" in project management, or the days before the quality movement where high quality was hit or miss. Both of the disciplines recognized the value of formal process and defined skills that would ensure the organization can systematically improve quality and ensure projects were accomplished on time and on budget. The same is possible for creating an Execution Focused Organization™.

Many studies have shown that organizations with a formal strategy execution process in place dramatically outperform organizations without one. In one study by IDC Research[28], 75% of those companies rated "most competitive" in their industry used a formal performance management methodology, compared to only 43% who were rated least competitive. In a similar study done by the Balanced Scorecard Collaborative Research, of those companies that outperformed their competition 70% followed a formal process and only 27% operated without a formal process[29].

Strategy Execution 3.0

How and why did strategy become part of our management processes? Strategy can be traced back to the earliest days of military operations. Sun Tzu's book, *The Art of War*, which dates back to the second century BC, is still considered by many as required reading for military and corporate leaders. But strategy did not become a formal part of leadership's role until early in the 20th century.

The first formal strategic planning for business was the Harvard Policy Model introduced in the 1920s. The main purpose was to help a firm develop the best fit between itself and its environment, to develop the best strategy for the firm. One of the major tools that came from this model was the well-known SWOT analysis. This could be considered first generation execution management.

Second generation execution management entered the scene around 1970 concurrent with the recognition of the importance of involving and aligning all the people in the organization. Policy Deployment or Hoshin Planning is a strategy management methodology based on the work of Professor Kaoru Ishikawa in the late 1950s. It is designed to use the collective thinking power of all employees to make their organization the best in its field. Hoshin planning added the importance of "cascading goals" throughout the organization to achieve focus, involvement and accountability in the strategic planning process.

In Figure 23 on the next page we see a second contribution to the strategy management methodology from The Quality Movement of 70s and 80s. Management used the Deming Cycle as a decision process for managing strategy implementation.

I consider the breakthroughs of Norton & Kaplan in The Balanced Scorecard as the pinnacle of second generation execution management.

I began working with The Balanced Scorecard in early 1993, shortly after it came out. Since I believed strongly that organizations are holistic systems and "what we measured is what we got," it seemed a natural fit.

As I worked with it though, I felt it was not addressing all of the forces operating in support of or in opposition to an organization's ability to execute. While it was a significant breakthrough, it quickly revealed its shortcomings to me.

I discovered that it was still rooted in the traditional left-brain, cause-effect orientation of the Activity field. It focused on what an organization does and how it does it. It did not include metrics for improving the Relationship field or the Context field nor did the methodology have any explicit way to factor in the interdependent relationships of the three fields.

As Sir Isaac Newton once said, "If I have seen a little further it is by standing on the shoulders of giants." I could only discover The Living Organization®, The Arc Framework® and The Real Time Execution™ System (RTE-S™) because of the work that has come before. Those who are familiar with *The Balanced Scorecard* (BSC) will have already noticed similar elements in The Living Organization® model.

We kept the four major activities all businesses need to manage – Financial, Customers, Process and People – and then advanced the body of knowledge. By seeing an organization as a living entity driven by the forces of Activity, Relationship and Context, we bring more of the process of creating results under control.

For example, in the BSC model Learning & Growth lumps Human Capital, Information Capital and Organization Capital together. In The Living Organization® model, each element has its own place so companies can properly evaluate and appropriately define and manage improvement initiatives.

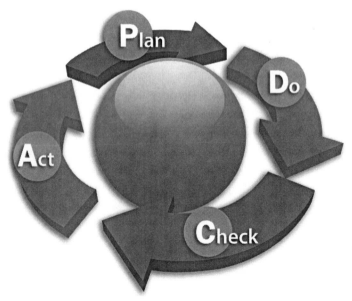

Figure 23

Management today orients itself towards one of three major schools of thought when setting up a decision framework. These are:

Quality Management: "A management approach, centered on quality, based on the participation of all organization members, aimed at long term success through customer satisfaction and benefits to organization members and society.[30]"

Shareholder Value: "The Shareholder's money should be used to earn a higher return than they could earn by investing in other assets with the same amount of risk[31]."

Performance Management: "A framework that translates an organization's strategy into a set of objectives and measures and aligns the organization to them through its planning and control process[32]." (Balanced Scorecard falls into this category)

Just as the four perspectives first introduced in the Balanced Scorecard are interdependent and one cannot take precedence over another, these decision-making models are equally interdependent. It is a mistake to assert that one is the dominant theme an organization should adopt for success. All three, quality, value creation, and performance management, are equally critical to the success of an organization. If you choose one over the other you run the risk of focusing your efforts on maximizing that dominant theme and potentially losing sight of the importance of the other two. It would be like a doctor focusing only on exercise and ignoring diet or lifestyle choices. In the long run if all three decision frameworks are not properly managed as interdependent parts of a whole system, the organization will sub-optimize its performance.

The Living Organization® model brings these perspectives into a single model. By seeing all results as a process of the transformation of energy, we integrate all activities to balance and maximize the flow of energy. We simultaneously maximize the quality of products and service, customer experience, employee experience, shareholder value, and our relationship to the environment whose resources we use. No one element can be out of balance if we are to achieve maximum results.

The final area we improved on is the inclusion of the three fields of energy: Activity, Relationship, and Context. As we discussed in the previous chapter, The ARC Framework® provides a way to identify the forces driving success and the forces hindering success. If we return to the force field analysis discussed in Chapter 1, we can see in Figure 24 below the benefit of identifying an organization's strength and weakness in each quadrant.

Whether you use force field analysis formally or not, you inherently always look to maximize the driving forces and minimize or eliminate the restraining forces.

This is the foundation of how strategic initiatives are decided. But what if you are not aware of some forces? Does that mean they are not operating?

Of course not, it only means that you cannot take any action to utilize them or minimize their negative impact. The result is that you will spend time and money to implement initiatives, usually Activity field initiatives, only to miss your schedule and waste resources as the unseen forces impede your progress.

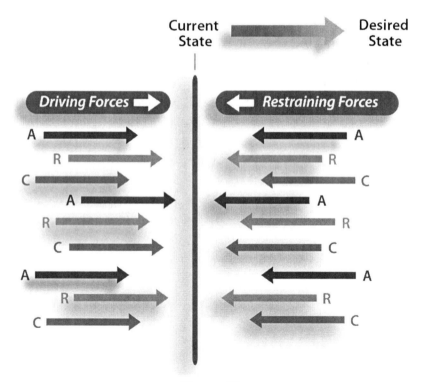

Figure 24

Of course not, it only means that you cannot take any action to utilize them or minimize their negative impact. The result is that you will spend time and money to implement initiatives, usually Activity field initiatives, only to miss your schedule and waste resources as the unseen forces impede your progress.

Strategic Planning is Dead – Long Live Strategy Execution

We opened this chapter with the classical vignette of the traditional strategic planning session. The current approach for defining where an organization is going and how it will get there - the ubiquitous Strategic Planning Offsite meeting - can no longer produce the desired result.

	Early 20th Century	21st Century
Geographic Reach	Local community (national at best)	Global community
Rate of Change	Change relatively slow (sometimes beyond the span of a life)	Change relatively slow (sometimes beyond the span of a life)
Product Life Cycles	Product life cycles measured in years, maybe decades	Product life cycles often measured in months
Degree of causality	Direct cause-effect relationships explained much (Scientific Management ruled)	Events seem to come out of nowhere – sense of random occurrence
Level of workforce education and skills	Labor force mostly unskilled	Labor force mostly educated, even for blue collar jobs
Employment relationship	Social contract	Meaning and Purpose
Predictability	Management can plan and predict with high degree of certainty	Plans are difficult to predict with any certainty
Competitive landscape	Competition within industry (well defined boundaries)	Industry boundaries are fluid – competition coming from anywhere
Speed of Communication	Slow	Almost Instantaneous
Level of complexity	Low- Moderate	Extreme

Figure 25

Why? In our dynamically changing world, the environment at the end of our planning horizon is not likely to be the same as the environment when we did the planning. The world that was once fairly stable, the world that gave rise to the strategic planning process, is not the world we live in today. The chart in Figure 25 on the previous page summarizes and illustrates many of those changes.

Clearly we operate in a world where the level of complexity has increased, as has the reach of our interactions. Our markets are broader and our customers are more sophisticated and demanding.

The speed of change has increased, as has the speed of communication. Competition can spring up from the most unlikely sources.

Who would have thought that Apple would compete with and threaten the record industry?

For most of the last century, the standard practice was to set a planning horizon, illustrated in Figure 26 below, usually 3 – 5 years, and define the desired outcome for that point in time. Under traditional wisdom you set your time horizon, you define your strategy plan, and hold to it so that you can focus on executing. Then 3 to 5 years later you redo the process.

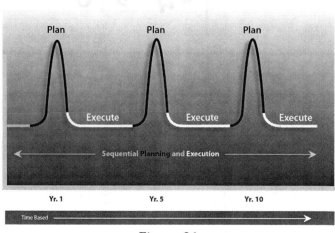

Figure 26

This approach was extremely viable during the first half of the 20th century primarily because the environment at the end of the planning horizon would be very much like it was at the beginning. A relatively stable environment provides an illusion of predictability and the ability to control our destiny. It looks like we can decide what we want and how to create it. By knowing how results were created in the past, we can pretty much plan how to create results in the future. We can set our plans and then execute them.

This began to break down during the latter half of the 20th century for the reasons illustrated in the table. The first decade of the 21st century has revealed very clearly that any such time-based approach to planning is no longer viable. We can no longer rely on that predictability and its cousin, control, to produce success.

Instead we need an approach that creates responsive interaction of the organization with its environment; when the environment changes, the organization changes naturally in response. Instead of predict and control, we must learn how to sense and respond.

This is how all organisms live and thrive and The Living Organization® model simply reflects how natural living organisms operate.

The diagram in Figure 27 shows the shift from a time based approach to a more fluid and responsive real time approach of integrating planning with execution.

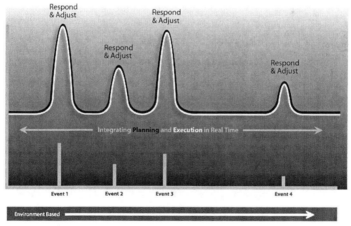

Figure 27

Start with a Compass!

While I believe that Strategic Planning is dead, I do not believe that setting a strategic direction is dead. The critical objective of all strategic planning is to establish the direction the organization will head. Without a clear understanding of where we are going, any path will get us there.

It is impossible in today's world to give people a clear map of how to get to the desired destination. For a map to work, the mapmakers need to have a degree of certainty about the territory that will be navigated. With the level of complexity and frequency of change happening in our world, no one individual or even an entire executive team can be that prescient.

The only workable solution is to provide every cell in our living system, the people of the organization, with a clear set of guidelines for making decisions on a minute-by-minute basis. We call that framework the Strategic Compass™. It has three components for setting a Context: the Soulful Purpose™, Vision of the Future and Core Values.

The original intent of Mission/Vision/Values was to achieve the very thing we have been discussing. The idea was to have a well-defined Mission/Vision/Value to deeply engage all employees, to energize and motivate them and to have a force that draws them into the future like a magnet. But most of the current efforts to achieve this have fallen far from this goal. The major reason is that most companies develop Mission/Vision/Values statements from an Activity perspective. Here are a couple of representative samples of mission/vision statements.

"We supply technically innovative software and hardware solutions to the OEM computer market that provide long-term benefits to our customers and our investors."

"To become the number one produce store by selling the highest quality, freshest farm produce, from farm to customer in under 24 hours on 75% of our range and with 98% customer satisfaction."

"To be the best developer of accounting software and grow our revenue by $255 million over 5 years."

Do you feel energized by such statements? Are these going to engage you and draw out a deep sense of passion and commitment to the organization's mission? My guess is that for most of you the answer is no. Statements like the ones above will never accomplish this. The simple reason is these speak mostly about what you do, the Activity field energy. This will generate some focus but only the energy of the Context field has that magnetic, energizing quality. Inspiration is not an activity we do; it is a connection with a deep meaningful reason for why we do what we do.

Certain companies have developed Mission/Vision/Values statements that are truly energizing. They have a clear sense of why they exist at their core. Their vision is a visual picture of what their world looks like as their Soulful Purpose™ unfolds and is more fully realized. Their Core Values are truly used to guide their behaviors. And they are not mere plaques on the wall but are felt deep within the whole corporate body. It is the "music" of the organization.

Soulful Purpose™

Understanding an organization's Soulful Purpose™ is not a simple matter of defining what we do and for whom. Rather it is connecting with the very essence of why the organization has come into being. This is somewhat easier to do during the startup phase. After an organization has been around for 10, 20, 40 or 100 years, it is easy to lose sight of why it exists.

One tool we use to help organizations discover their Soulful Purpose™ is to ask the "It's a Wonderful Life" question. Many people have seen the classic movie traditionally shown around Christmas in the United States. It stars Jimmy Stewart, who feels his life is useless and meaningless. He is shown by an angel what the world would be like if he was not in it. At the end he discovers his life does have meaning and purpose and he knows the unique gifts he is meant to bring.

Like people, all organizations have a unique meaning and purpose that you can discover by asking the question, "What would the world be missing if this organization didn't exist?" The answer will emerge as a series of stories that you want to capture. Do not try to create a "mission statement" and do not turn the Soulful Purpose™ into a simple plaque to be hung in the lobby of your organization. Rather capture and communicate the richness that lies in the story that conveys why the organization exits.

Context field is a high-energy field that is given form by the stories we tell. Your Soulful Purpose™ is captured by the stories you and others within your organization tell of how you contribute to your customers and the way those stories move people. Here are a few examples.

A company that developed flight control systems for the F-14 was having an all-hands meeting. A pilot in full flight suit walks in and is introduced as a Navy pilot just back from Iraq. The pilot shared how he was flying a mission over northern Iraq when his plane was hit. He stood before all the employees today because of the work each one of them did. If it wasn't for how perfectly that company's flight control systems worked, he would never have made it back to the ship. He was alive today because of what they did every day, each and every one of them.

An engineering services company that tests products to ensure they are performing within specs does work for aerospace firms, the Department of Defense, the automotive industry, and the telecommunications industry among others. In preparing for a presentation to Boeing, the COO realized how many of the Boeing suppliers they have supported. In fact he discovered that 80% of products used in the new Boeing 787 Dreamliner passed through their labs. As he visited each facility to share their strategic direction, he shared this story. He then added, "You can rest assured that when you, your family and friends fly on the new 787 Dreamliner, they will come home safely because of the work each of you do."

A friend of mine who used to work at Edwards Lifesciences shared this story with me. Edwards sells heart stents among other medical devices. Stents are devices that are used to keep collapsing vessels open to allow the flow of blood. To ensure that everyone in the organization knew the real reason they existed, the CEO would periodically bring in an individual who has one of their stents. As he toured the former heart patient through the facility he would introduce him or her to the employees in various departments. Then he would turn to each employee and say, "The work you do saved this person's life. Never think for one moment that what you do is not important or that you do not make a difference."

These examples are just a few among thousands out there. Every organization exists to do more than make money, increase market share, or be the best in their field. The do more than just sell goods or services to customers. They make a difference. They have a Soulful Purpose™. What's yours?

The Mission

Many think of the mission as the same as the purpose. Perhaps I am splitting hairs but I think it is important to differentiate the Soulful Purpose™ from the Mission of the organization. The Soulful Purpose™ is the core reason an organization exists, this defines the unique contribution it is meant to make and it is the foundation on which the stories that define the meaning and purpose of organization are built.

Any particular purpose can be expressed in many different ways. For example, I might have the sense of purpose to help green the planet. I can choose many paths to contribute to this purpose. I can decide to join in the efforts for reforestation of the planet's rainforests. I can decide to focus on the creation of urban greenbelts and parks. I can choose to build nurseries that focus on helping people create private gardens. All of these are viable expressions of the Soulful Purpose™ of greening our planet.

Each company not only has a particular Soulful Purpose™, it will also choose a particular mission that allows it to express that purpose. Soulful Purpose™ is why we are doing what we are doing and the Mission is how we express our purpose.

Future Vision

Once you clearly know why your organization exists and what contribution it is meant to bring into the world, you can ask the question, "What would the world look like in 3, 5 or 10 years if your Soulful Purpose™ was more fully realized?" Again, this is different than the more common vision statements that we see hanging on the walls of corporate lobbies, the ones that say it is our vision to be the best, the biggest or the leading company in our industry.

The future vision is a story, one that is imagined, dreamed, and created out of a collective desire to see it become so. Remember, everything is energy, the table is energy, the chair is energy, and your computer is energy.

A tree is energy, you are energy, and your company is energy. The difference between energy in the form of a living organism versus other forms of energy is that living organisms transform energy - they create! The difference between viewing your company as a Living Organization® versus viewing it as a machine of production is that machines do not create, they merely produce.

When organizations create as an expression of the Soulful Purpose™, they experience a flow and ease to their efforts similar to the ease and flow individuals experience when they create the results they are meant to create. It feels as if they are effortlessly manifesting magical results.

The future vision is the story of your Soulful Purpose™ unfolding. When defining the picture of the future, it is useful to look at the whole corporate body. You can approach this by asking, "When our Soulful Purpose™ is more fully realized, what will customers experience, what will our people experience, what is the nature of our leadership team, how will we operate, and what will be the measurable results?" In other words define each element of The Living Organization® - Leadership, People, Process, Customers, in each of the three fields of energy - Activity, Relationship, and Context.

Core Values

Core Values are those deeply held beliefs that are inviolate. Though behaviors may not always be in accordance with them (organizations are only human after all), the organization is fully committed to stand behind them. It is important to establish your Aspiration Core Values. This is likely to be different from your actual lived core values and this is absolutely perfect. As with the development and growth of individuals, an organization must set its sights on what it aspires to become. It is in closing the gap between what we aspire to and what we actually are that sets in motion the process of transforming energy.

Since there is always a gap between aspired core values and lived core values, the real question is not why a corporation behaved out of integrity with its core values but rather what does it do when it discovers such behavior. Do they rationalize the behaviors or do they move quickly to regain alignment? By honestly observing and using our actual behaviors as a mirror of who we are truly being, we create an opportunity to go to the next stage of organizational development.

Like a person, an organization can become conscious. It starts by defining what it wants to stand for and works to remain conscious of when it is living in accordance with its beliefs and its core values and when it is not. Just as a person grows and becomes conscious when they understand what in their unconscious is driving them to behave inconsistently with their core values, so too will an organization move from unconsciousness to a conscious organization.

Such an organization is aware of why it is here and what it is meant to contribute. It knows its purpose and how it is to serve. It lives to be in service to all of its constituencies. It knows what it stands for and creatively works with its environment to create a future consistent with its deeper purpose. A conscious organization knows when it is not operating within integrity and quickly realigns itself, using those moments as opportunities to learn about and integrate more of its purpose.

Living a conscious life is consistent with achieving results. Leadership's role is to bring themselves and the organization into alignment with their deeper purpose and core values on the path towards its goals. This is the path to achieving the kind of magical results we opened the book with. The key is having a system for creating the desired results that reveals all the forces impacting success and allows appropriate actions to be taken for each of those forces.

Alignment is the key

Setting the direction is the first step. Without a compass, the organization will wonder from opportunity to opportunity reacting instead of creating. And once we know where we are going, then we must get everyone to go in that direction. The whole organization must be aligned so that everyone has the same line of sight in the same strategic direction.

To better understand the power of alignment, let's continue the analogy that the corporate body operates in a similar fashion to the human body. We know that over 90% of our behavioral responses to our environment occur semi-autonomously. The nervous system determines the body's response to thousands upon thousands of simultaneous inputs received from our environment. The brain (our body's central decision making center) has very little say about how our body responds most of the time.

The fact that much of our organization's behavior has become unconscious is mostly a good thing; it has been incorporated in the semi-autonomic nervous system of the corporate body. Imagine what life would be like if all decisions had to first go to our brains for a decision before any action could occur. There are thousands, perhaps millions of choices being made between the many functional parts of our bodies in one of the most coordinated and collaborative team efforts one can imagine.

It's a lot like learning to ride a bike. Eventually we become proficient because most of the rules for riding and balancing have become part of our unconscious, part of our semi-autonomic nervous system. This is what allows an organization to operate with a high degree of efficiency. It is also what makes changing the basic rules for how we operate so difficult and why we have to make those rules conscious once again.

What we call resistance to change is really nothing more than energy that has formed very strong flow patterns. Our organization only appears to be resistant to change because these energy patterns usually remain under the surface of what we pay attention to.

Think about what happens when you drive on the freeway at 65 mph. How much of your conscious thought is focused on driving? What percentage of your brain is coordinating your foot, which is pressing on the pedal, or your arm which controls the steering wheel? Imagine the vast number of data points supplied to the processor in your brain from your eyes as they scan the environment around you. All this is going on while our conscious thoughts are focused on everything but our driving. It is quite amazing that we ever get to our destination, let alone get there safely.

In the traditional approach to strategic execution, the CEO and executive team participate in an offsite planning session where they evaluate strengths, weaknesses, opportunities and threats, (the classic SWOT analysis), set the future direction for the organization, and map out specific action plans that they believe will achieve the desired results. They then go back and communicate these well thought-out plans to the rest of the organization with "marching orders" listing what the various functional departments will do.

This approach puts a lot of emphasis on the executive team (the brain of the corporate body), and forces it to remain heavily involved in decision making. Starting with the planning process and carrying over into the myriad day-to-day decisions, the executive team remains the dominant decision maker. When the environment moved slower this was acceptable but at today's rate of change this no longer works. It is analogous to the brain guiding every movement while driving a car. The driver would slow down to the same speed as a student driver trying to get everything coordinated.

Wouldn't it be nice if our organizations could get us to our destination with the same degree of semi-autonomous behavior as our bodies do while driving a car? What if your corporate body could respond to a rapidly changing environment with the speedy and accurate decisions that ensure our ultimate success, much as the human body gets us to our destination?

The solution lies in understanding the nature of decision-making: every decision is made within a specific context. When we face a choice, we evaluate the various options against a defined set of criteria. We do this so rapidly we are not aware of it but in fact every decision is made within a defined context. This context holds three major pieces of information. The first is what we came here to do (as best as we understand it at the moment), which is the contribution we are uniquely gifted to make, our Soulful Purpose™. The second is the values that define what we stand for, which are the beliefs we hold so dear we could not possibly violate them. The final component defines where we are going, the results of our Soulful Purpose™ expressed. With these three key parameters, making a choice is quick, easy and straightforward.

In the current approach to strategic planning, a well executed off-site meeting will establish a Context for the organization that is strong and powerful and will act as the compass for the executives as they move forward. Unfortunately that is where it typically resides, with the Executive Team. Little, if anything is ever done to infuse this core Context throughout the organization. Instead, the executives usually communicate only the "what and the how" of the plan (Activity), not the "where and why (Context)."

Without the Context for sorting and evaluating input, the corporate body will never be able to execute without continuous involvement from the executives. Going back to our driving example, most organizations today operate like student drivers who think about every move they make. Or worse yet, everyone in the organization makes rapid decisions based on a variety of contexts, none of them well aligned. Either way the execution is slowed way down.

To function at the speed of today's business environment, the corporate body must operate in a semi-autonomous fashion, much like the human body.

This requires a different approach to strategic planning, with most planning focusing on establishing a strong Context that goes beyond being merely communicated: it is deeply infused throughout the corporate nervous system. What is communicated goes beyond the usual "what and the how" of the plan, and includes the deeper more meaningful "where and why."

When every individual (the living cells of the corporate body) is infused with the right Context for making decisions, then like our bodies when driving the car, they will respond in appropriate alignment and make the right decisions.

The title, the lyrics and the music

We have stressed that the elements of The Strategic Compass™ are not the simple mission, vision, values statements we have all become familiar with. Yet at some time, the work of defining the elements of Soulful Purpose™ Mission, Core Values and Future Vision will be reduced to a set of statements that will be passed around the organization. It will be up to the leaders to keep the impact of the Soulful Purpose™ alive in people's minds.

Remember that statements hung on the wall do not generate the energy that creates passion, engagement and alignment, only the stories that carry the Context Energy can do that. If we think of how songs impact us, we can recognize how to have it all.

A song title does nothing to create the emotional connection we have with a song. Neither do the lyrics alone, although they are much more powerful than just the title. It is the combination of the music and the lyrics that creates our emotional attachment to a song. So much so that many years can go by without hearing the song and the minute we hear the first few bars, we are immediately reconnected with the experience. We can even hear someone mention the title of the song and our minds will begin to replay it with its full emotional impact.

The stories we tell with the full range of emotions behind them are the combination of the lyrics and the music. When our organization fully embodies the story, then the title of the song will carry the full impact of the song itself. The statements that will eventually be passed around and hung on the office walls will evoke the song, the lyrics and music that are represented by the title.

Executing in Real Time

All execution management systems rely on the basic formulas of knowing where you are, defining where you want to go, and deciding on a path to get there. As you move toward your desired goal, it is also necessary to track your progress and make adjustments if you are trending off target.

Real Time Execution System™ (RTE-S™)

This is the same approach we use in the Real Time Execution System™ (RTE-S™), the performance and execution management process for The Living Organization®. It follows the "Plan – Do – Check – Act" of Deming's quality process discussed earlier.

In the RTE-S™ model shown in Figure 28 on the next page we have six basic steps: Define, Assess, Decide, Perform, Evaluate and Align. Unlike other systems, we place Define in the center of the action. This is done for two reasons. First, it is not merely a step in a cyclical process but rather it sets the direction and the context for all decisions. It is in essence the Strategic Compass™. All other components of the system rely on this compass as the center of all decisions and choices. Similarly Align is also not a step in decision making as much as it is the boundary conditions within which decisions are made.

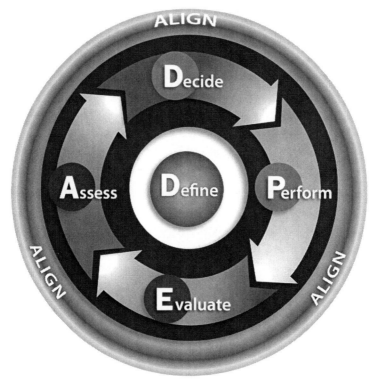

Figure 28

It's about time

In our approach, we include time as a critical function of the process. One of the beautiful aspects of business is that it is time based. When we establish goals, we set a time frame for when the goal is to be accomplished. When we calculate Return on Investment, time is an important component of the equation. Time is an important component for development as well. It sets in motion the change process that brings about the challenges that invoke our development. Without time, there would be no forward motion. Everything in business, and in life, is about time.

The diagram in Figure 29 on the next page shows the six steps of the Real Time Execution System™ along the time dimension. We see that our circle is now represented by a wave function.

From this perspective we can further see the importance of the Strategic Compass™. First, it sets the direction of the organization's efforts.

The Strategic Compass™ is the central vector around which energy flows. The Soulful Purpose™, along with the Future Vision, directs the flow of all Activity and energy transformation. It acts as wave-guides for the transformation of energy. It sets the boundaries for the behaviors of all the cells of the corporate body.

Also notice in this diagram that the frequency of the wave defines the speed of execution. The rise time of the Assess segment is directly proportional to the organization's ability to accurately assess its position relative to its environment. The Decide phase orients the organization to what it will do in response to its environment; the more accurate the assessment the more accurate the response. Perform is the act of releasing the energy, transforming it into the desired outcome. As with all physical systems, the amount of energy that can be released is a function of the potential energy stored in the system. The amplitude represents the amount of potential energy derived from drawing on all the forces of the Relationship and Context fields and applying it to the Activity of the Perform phase. Finally, the Evaluate phase sets the stage for the necessary midcourse correction and triggers the next cycle.

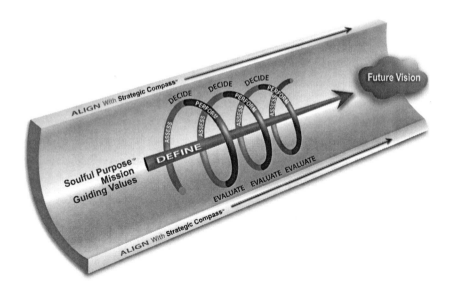

Figure 29

Alignment

The second benefit of a strong Strategic Compass™ is that it sets the boundaries for behaviors and serves as the foundation for aligning the organization and does it in a way that opens the creative forces of the organization rather than shuts them down.

In the traditional approach to alignment, goals are established at the top and cascade down to the rest of the organization. This top-down process tells the people in the organization what is to be done and at times even tells them how to do it. This has the side effect of constraining individual and organizational creativity.

By establishing a Strategic Compass™, ingraining it within everyone as part of their personal context, you create room for each individual to respond to the challenges they face with the utmost freedom for creativity while still retaining focused execution.

I once attended a workshop where the presenter told a story about the U.S. Constitution. He explained that after much debate over the framing of the constitution, the real power lay in the simplicity of the Bill of Rights, the first ten amendments. Each one of them begins with "Congress shall not…" The comment he made that day impressed me. "Because it set the boundaries of what we could not do, everything else was possible." He went on to remind us that the last five commandments of the 10 commandments also start with "thou shall not…"

It was easy for me to see how this applied to organizations. Rather than set up a lot of procedures to tell people what they are supposed to do and how they should act, what if we simply told them the boundaries that they could not cross. That leaves a lot of room for them to decide how best to accomplish what they were hired to accomplish. In other words, a creative environment is best achieved when the boundaries are clear and individuals are allowed to choose whatever approach they feel best achieves the objectives that lie within the boundary.

Alignment surrounds the activity cycle of Assess-Decide-Perform-Evaluate. Drawing strongly on the Strategic Compass™, alignment is the process of establishing the boundary conditions within which freedom of action is allowed. The key elements of alignment are:

Goal Alignment – Goals are the metrics we use to inform us of our progress and if we are on track to our desired results. Goal alignment means that each business unit, functional department and individual's goals represent their contribution to the overall effort. This is achieved through the alignment of each unit's objectives, metrics and targets. Each unit knows how their results contribute to The Living Organization® unit it is part of starting with the individual moving up to the team(s) then to the department and ultimately to the organization. This relates to Activity field Alignment.

Infrastructure alignment – An organization is supported by many systems that define how work gets done. These systems traditionally have evolved from previous stages of the organization's life cycle and can become calcified. The often-heard comment "we do it this way because that is the way it has always been done" is the symptom of an organization whose infrastructure is now defining its behaviors rather than supporting them. Infrastructure alignment is directly related to Relationship field alignment.

Cultural Alignment – Perhaps the most important and often overlooked component is the need to align the culture of the organization with the strategy. Like infrastructure, culture evolves over time, carrying with it the good and bad of previous stages of the company's history. Culture is the key element of the Context field; and as we will explain below, all activity will be limited to only those actions supported by the culture. This is the alignment related to the organization's Context field.

	Leadership	People	Processes & Business Model	Customers & Suppliers
A	Management	Technical Skills	Workflow & Metrics	Needs & Solutions
R	Teams & Collaboration	Interpersonal Skills	Orgainization Design & Information Flow	Brand & Reputation
C	Motivation & Inspiration	Intrapersonal Skills	Culture, Norms & Rules	Trend Dynamics

Figure 30

Commitment Alignment – The organization will execute its strategy in direct proportion to the level of commitment the collective organization holds. It is critical to determine the level of commitment and to keep deepening it to accelerate the speed of execution. One of the strongest ways to get commitment is to give people choice. Choice empowers people. When they choose to commit to the Strategic Compass™, their level of commitment will rise proportionately. So will their level of engagement and passion. That is why Commitment Alignment is related to the individual's Context field.

Know your Place

All living creative organisms are in relationship with their environment. They know their capabilities and the factors in the environment that will impact their ability to create their desired outcome. They operate in concert with their environment, drawing resources from it and giving back to it to maintain balance. Organizations are no different. The organizations that know their capabilities and their place within the total ecosystem will, like all living beings, outperform those that don't. This is the purpose of the Assess phase of RTE-S™.

Using The ARC Framework® described in the previous chapter and shown on the previous page in Figure 30 allows an organization to get a richer picture of the capabilities they can draw on. It also allows them to get a clearer picture of the environment they operate in and the deep trends of the total ecosystem. It is the traditional SWOT analysis from Execution 1.0 expanded to provide a more robust view of all the forces impacting success.

What to do, what to do?

Now that the organization is armed with information about its environment and its own strengths and weaknesses, it can decide the next course of action to move it closer to its desired outcomes. It can define a roadmap for the next phase of Execution, how best to close the gap between the desired state and the current state. The Decide phase establishes strategic themes, the execution map, and strategic initiatives and establishes the strategy investment (StratEx) budget.

Figure 31

Developing the execution roadmap must take into account the relationship of Activity, Relationship and Context fields as described earlier.

The activities an organization can perform are within, and supported by the Relationship and Context fields. An Activity that is outside those fields cannot be accomplished no matter how much effort is applied without first expanding the other two fields to include the new Activity. This is one of the critical aspects that make RTE-S™ a management system that will save time and money.

When defining the initiatives and their sequence of execution, it is critical to take into account the interdependencies of the energy fields. Recall the relationships of Activity, Relationship, and Context as we discussed in Chapter 9 and shown again in Figure 31 above. If a desired outcome requires a change in activity that is outside the Context Field domain, then an explicit initiative to reweave the stories that define the context boundaries must be a precedent or least a parallel initiative. Appropriate resources must be allocated to this initiative to ensure its successful completion. If this is overlooked, as it all too often is, the company will waste time and money trying to implement a change in activity that cannot be successfully implemented.

The outcome is a roadmap and a scorecard for guiding and managing the execution. Like any roadmap, it provides the direction for the journey and key mileposts along the way to ensure you stay on track to the destination. The Execution Map™ shown in Figure 32 on the next page provides a framework for tying together all of the elements of the Real Time Execution System™ and provides a map to navigate your journey. The Strategic Compass™ sets the direction. The objectives for each of the key domains provide the guideposts along the way.

The Execution Scorecard™ translates the map into a set of specific initiatives to execute and also identifies responsibilities, metrics, targets and required investments. The scorecard initiatives are the most likely path as can be best determined at the beginning of the journey.

The Evaluate and Assess phases will ensure that the initiatives being performed remain appropriate to the constantly changing environment.

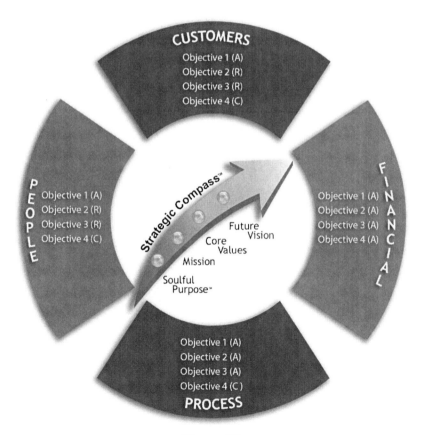

Figure 32

Get ready the future is coming

Strategy is all about the future so strategy execution has to be more than simply getting things done. Another way to view strategy is that it prepares the organization to meet the demands of the future it is creating. In other words, it is a developmental act.

Like the development of a person, we must pay attention to the skills the organization has, which reflect its ability to perform in the Activity field. We can also easily recognize the importance of the relationships it has with all of its stakeholders, customers, suppliers, employees, investors, etc. What may not be so obvious is the importance of determining the organization's collective Emotional Intelligence (EQ).

EQ has become a fairly common skill dimension when dealing with individuals. It has been shown repeatedly that EQ is considerably more important to an individual's success then their knowledge or functional skill set. Emotional Intelligence, described earlier in more detail, can be summarized to cover four skill domains – Self-Awareness, Self-Management, Social-Awareness, and Relationship-Management. You can also evaluate the collective Emotional Intelligence of organizations along the same four domains.

To illustrate, have you ever witnessed an organization respond to a change in conditions in a way that resembles a childlike outburst, or go into a collective state of depression when something significant happens? A client in the food services industry brought me in because the organization as a whole was not performing and there was no apparent reason why it shouldn't be. During the assessment phase I uncovered a deep sense of grief pervading most of the executives and managers. Not that anyone specifically stated this; rather it showed up in what they weren't saying and how they were talking. I saw the same signs an individual exhibits when going through a death and mourning process.

It turned out that the organization had undergone significant re-organization and everyone was experiencing the loss, the "death" of the way things used to be. The first thing we did prior to the rest of the off-site agenda was to conduct a mourning ceremony. It was a simple process. Everyone lined up by his or her length of service and each one described the way the organization was at the time the first joined the company. We went from the birth of the company to the current day. This process allowed the collective to remember and honor what had come before, to let it go, and then open to the creation of what was to come. Organizations as collectives process emotions the same way an individual does.

As with emotional intelligence, which measures the skills of an individual and an organization with Relationship energy, we need to determine an individual's and an organization's ability to operate within the Context field. Also discussed earlier, this is much interest in Spiritual Intelligence, the ability to work with one's sense of meaning and purpose. Thanks to the work of Cindy Wigglesworth, we now have an assessment instrument, the Spiritual Intelligence Inventory (SQi) that also determines skills in four domains. For SQi those domains are – Self/Ego-Awareness, Universal-Awareness, Self-Mastery, and Social-Mastery/Presence.

The point is clear. Like helping an individual grow, develop and mature, preparing an organization for the future is a process of working with all the skills associated with Activity, Relationship and Context. Like an individual, if an organization's development is stifled, it will limit how much it can contribute and produce. When I coach individuals who want to improve their lives, we define the needed functional skills that the new desired lives would require. I also work with them to improve their interpersonal skills so they could build the networks and relationships they will need to support their new life. And I work with them on the beliefs that might sabotage all of their other efforts if not properly addressed. If this is required to significantly improve an individual's life, why would the same three domains of developmental effort not be required for an organization?

Incrementing or Innovating – It makes a difference

Does your strategic direction call for incremental improvement of your current business or are you setting out on a new innovative approach to serving your customers? There is a distinct difference between the two, one that will significantly change the challenges of execution.

The best way to understand the difference is to think of your organization as a simple manufacturing production line. A production line is set up to produce a certain product and is optimized to produce that product in the most efficient way possible. When it is time to produce a different product, the production line is stopped and retooled for the new product.

Your company, like a production line, has been fine tuned to produce the goods and services for the customers you serve. Every aspect of your company from engineering to finance, from operations to sales has evolved over time to make the production of the goods and services you produce as optimal as possible. You have developed certain norms, rules, metrics and even a culture that has created your success. Achieving your operating objectives is akin to meeting production goals in the "production line" metaphor.

If your plans call for little or no change to the basic way you are operating, your strategy will simply call for incremental improvements of your existing "production line." You may add a new tool such as implementing an ERP system, or improve the training of the people in various departments, but your basic production line, the fundamental way you operate, is not going to change. Strategy planning in this scenario is an Incremental Strategy, strategies to improve on the existing way we do business.

But let's now look at a different type of strategy, an Innovation Strategy. Examples of an Innovation Strategic Direction would be moving up the value chain, serving different customers in a different way, offering a higher value-added set of products and services, or moving from a product oriented business to a service dominated business (or vice versa).

These changes in strategic direction require a shift in how you will do business in the future. If, for example, you are moving from selling a technical product to engineers to selling a solution to corporate executives, you will likely be dealing with longer sales cycles, different approaches to determining the product roadmap and different methods for reaching the market. You might even be facing a different revenue model. In essence the norms, rules, structures, and business models that you have used to create success will all have to change.

In terms of our metaphor you will be retooling the organizational "production line." But unlike a manufacturing operation, you cannot shut down the existing production line to retool it. Executing an Innovation Strategy requires retooling the organization production line while the existing production line is still operating.

Who's changing what?

Strategy is about improving the way things are being done; strategy is about change. Whether it is incremental or innovative, as shown in Figure 33 below, managing strategy execution is managing change.

As the diagram shows, even incremental strategy has a slope to it, meaning that some change management is going to be called for. To increase performance over time, either path requires changes in how the organization operates. Yet clearly, the change management process for an innovative strategy will be much more significant than for an incremental strategy.

For many companies, strategic plans are incremental in nature and very close to operating plans. These are mostly plans to improve operating effectiveness and extend the current business model. When you are setting a strategic direction that is innovative, trying to manage the strategy execution the same way will be devastating and unlikely to succeed.

What determines an innovation strategy is the degree by which you are making changes to the basic business model. This model is the norms, rules, metrics and processes of how the organization produces its results[33].

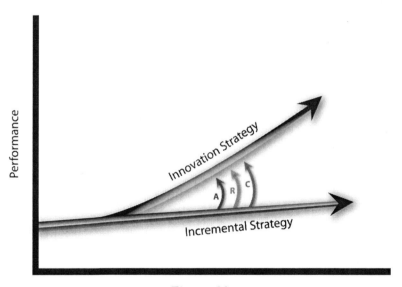

Figure 33

Because Innovation strategy is changing the fundamental way "things are done around here" it requires a different focus. Innovative Strategy must take into account the forces within your organization that are operating mostly under the surface at the unconscious level; the forces that have established the existing boundaries that everyone has become comfortable with. Where Incremental Strategy will likely deal with the forces associated with the Activity Field, Innovation Strategy requires reweaving the boundaries of the Context Field and redefining the Relationship Field.

It is during the innovative shifts in strategy that the Context and Relationship Fields have the most impact. If you remain unconscious to them, they could very well work against you. However if you include specific strategic initiatives to reframe them, they will carry you on a wave of success.

To manage the execution of an Innovation Strategy, specific initiatives with objective, metrics and targets must be identified. This provides the ability to track what has heretofore been seen as the soft and mushy side of business. It makes the soft side hard and measurable. Often slight changes in the patterns of relationship energy and context energy, the energy that defines our meaning and purpose, will create significant changes in results.

What's your horizon?

If strategy is a developmental process, then certain actions must be included in this year's efforts that will lay a foundation for what is required in the future. A simple example is the difference between business development and sales. We all know Sales is focused on getting current period business, whether daily, monthly, quarterly, or annually. Their focus is on finding opportunities and closing the business.

Business development, on the other hand, focuses on building opportunities that will turn into sales in the future. For example, a client in the education field wanted to establish a strong international presence and set a strategic objective to increase their international business to equal their domestic business. They had very little presence in international markets nor did they have a lot of experience building international channels. Their first strategic initiative was to hire a senior business development person who had international experience. They gave that person a three-year charter to build relationships, develop channels, and create a pipeline of opportunities. You can see how each element of the charter builds on the previous.

There are three major time horizons, H1 is current activities we will execute this year, H2 is an intermediate stage, what we will be working on in two to three years, and H3 is the point in the future where we have reached our desired new capability, typically three to five or more years. To achieve the goals set for H3 (have international revenues equal domestic revenues), we must set intermediate goals for H2 (develop the channel and increase opportunities), and foundation laying goals for H1 (hire an international development person).

For most people this will seem obvious. I wish it were so. All too often we experience companies that set goals for Horizon 3 and do not think through what has to be changed to get them there. They believe too strongly in the maxim, "Set the targets and the rest will take care of itself." While that is true for some people and for some organizations, it is not true for everyone. Some people can figure it out on their own while others cannot. Do not slip into the trap of thinking this is because of differences in intelligence. It is a difference in developmental maturity.

Those individuals who are higher on the developmental scale tend to operate well on their own. This might seem intuitive but what might not be readily apparent is that a person who is higher in SQ skills and low in functional abilities will be more capable of working with broadly defined objectives and goals than a person with high functional skills but low SQ skills. The same is true for an organization.

Proper preparation requires proper development and sequencing of Activity, Relationship and Context. Remember the example above about the desire to improve the win ratio. Before any Activity field changes can take hold, change to the Context field was required. The Context field is slowest of the three to change, with Relationship next and Activity the quickest to change (assuming the other two support the change).

When developing the strategic initiatives to prepare the organization for the future, one must assign to Horizon 1, 2 and 3 the appropriate Activity, Relationship and Context goals and objectives and recognize their interdependence.

Put your money where your mouth is

It is one thing to establish a set of initiatives needed to prepare the organization for the future but are you committing to them? Anything that is going to get done requires a commitment and commitment is demonstrated by the allocation of resources.

Ask any Human Resource executive about the strategic development of people. How many times have you sat through a strategic planning session where the objective is "ensure we develop our people, they are our most important asset?" Then when budgets are established or expenses are cut the first thing to go is the training and development budget.

It seems there is a common virus running through most corporations, the viral infection of urgentitis. It seems we will always respond to what is right in front of us, the "urgent and immediate," at the expense of what is important to prepare us for the future. And one of the side effects of this virus is that it erases our memories so that we can't understand why we aren't accomplishing our goals.

There are four critical steps for the Decide Phase:

Determine the strategic initiatives

Sequence the initiatives

Select the metrics and set the targets

Allocate the resources.

When it comes to allocating resources it is important that strategy initiatives, especially horizon 2 and 3 initiatives, have a clearly established budget. A concept that has evolved with the Balanced Scorecard approach that we carry forward into RTE-S™ is the establishment of a StratEx budget.

StratEx can be thought of similar to CapEx budgets. Most organizations recognize that they need to establish a separate budget for capital expenditures. This budget typically covers expenditures to acquire new equipment and funds for the ongoing maintenance of existing capital. Similarly a StratEx budget ensures that resources are allocated to appropriate investments for strategy initiative execution. Without this, the organization will quickly recognize that there is no commitment to strategy and will revert to growth through "crisis of the day" management.

The executive team will consider strategy as nothing more than a fun weekend off-site that will produce nothing substantial.

Who dreamed this up anyway?

As we said, strategy is the process of creating the future. We can view the future as a continuation of the past or as a creative act of deciding what we want the future to be. We know from life that living entities are oriented towards creation. It is what makes living entities different from machines. We dream of what is possible and then set out to make it so. Setting your vision of the future is setting into motion the realization of a dream. Ask any entrepreneur when they started; they had a dream of something they thought was possible when no one else did. It is the process of dreaming and then following that dream that makes life that much richer. This is true for you and it is true for your organization.

While we strongly believe the process of defining the future is a creative process there is a role for looking to the past as part of the process. By understanding the patterns of the past we can gain insight into the momentum and direction of the energy flow as it moves towards the future.

The foundational premise that everything is energy would dictate that current reality is the energy that has evolved from the transformation of the energy of the past. Trends are nothing more than energy momentum, deep patterns that reveal which way things are heading. The more momentum a trend has the stronger the energy pattern and the more energy it will take to change it.

Most people recognize the concept of an idea that was ahead of its time. The proper way to view this is that an idea at an early stage is a seed planted in the energy field of existing patterns of behavior. If the seed is hearty, it will attract more and more energy to it. As it does so, it begins to create new patterns of energy, which translate into new behaviors on the part of what is commonly called the innovators. If it demonstrates value, it will collect more and more energy and at a certain point, the tipping point, it will seem as if a new trend has emerged.

Understanding the trends of the past will help define how much energy is required to transform the current reality into the dream of the future you want to create. The future is never determined by the past.

The past only dictates the amount of energy the dream for a better future will require.

When deciding your strategic direction, you will choose a combination of following existing trends and innovating new trends. The ratio of this combination will depend on your Soulful Purpose™. If at your core you are a technological innovator you will obviously tend to be heavier on the side of innovating new trends. If you are a fast follower, you would be more oriented towards existing trends.

What did you assume?

Whichever role you choose, when it comes to selecting a set of strategic initiatives you will be making decisions based on a set of assumptions. Since strategy is about creating the future, all decisions will be based on the assumptions you make about past trends and future trends. It is extremely important to ensure that you capture all assumptions. Too often we see organizations make decisions based on assumptions that they think reflect reality.

As time goes on this reality bias will blind an organization to what is really transpiring in their environment. This will slow down or worse yet, eliminate the appropriate response to a changing environment. By documenting and tracking assumptions and continually asking during the Evaluate phase whether those assumptions are valid, an organization will naturally become more responsive to a dynamically changing world. As the saying goes, it is dangerous to drink one's own Kool-Aid.

Lights, Cameras, Action

Now that we have determined the theme of the corporate story and have outlined the script of the play, it is time to perform. It is time to get on the stage of life and put into action what we have planned.

Like all good performances, the actors need to understand their roles and how the play is intended to unfold. The process shifts to aligning the organization for action. Rather than think of the play as a fully scripted performance, think of it more like an improvisation performance.

Since today's world is defined by the rapidity of changes we are experiencing, we cannot define for our band of performers exactly what they will face and how they should respond. Rather we want each member of our troupe to understand the role they play and to have the skill to receive what the world offers and to respond in ways that move the play in the right direction.

This is what improv performers do. At any point in time they have no way of knowing what the other performers will say or do. They wait for the story to unfold. When an action is offered, the actor will respond to it. One of the key rules of improv is that you always accept the offer and the action and add your piece to it. This moves the play forward and becomes the next offer for another actor to step forward, accept, and add to.

I have had the great fortune that my wife, Jane, has spent over a decade performing a type of improv called Playback Theater. It starts with a member of the audience telling the outline of a story. The actors play that story back from the outline. The improv process defines what actually unfolds and that is almost always something magical.

I have come to see the same pattern applying to a corporation's desire to create its own future. The company has a story outline they want to manifest. However, the actual path to planned result rarely follows the expected path. Rather a natural fluid dance emerges between the organization and the events it is called on to respond to. How it responds makes all the difference in how the rest of the story unfolds. Learning the skills of improv will enhance the ultimate performance of the organization and create the same magic that emerges from a good improv performance.

Being able to respond to whatever the environment offers frees the creativity of the organization. Imagine if all the individual performers, the potential thousands of individuals on the corporate stage, had these abilities.

They would have the freedom to respond to the events that come across their desks in their own unique and creative way. The overall performance of the collective acting troupe will be a magical story of fulfilling the organization's Soulful Purpose™ in service to its customers.

Well, how did you do?

Peter Senge, in his 1990 book *The Fifth Discipline* brought the seminal idea of the learning organization into the limelight. To quote from his book, Senge says learning organizations are:

...organizations where people continually expand their capacity to create the results they truly desire, where new and expansive patterns of thinking are nurtured, where collective aspiration is set free, and where people are continually learning to see the whole together.

Arie de Geus, a follower of Senge, in his book *The Living Company*, underscores the importance of a learning organization. In his role as head of planning for Royal Dutch Shell, he explored why most companies die before their time and why a few seem to be able to continue on for hundreds of years. He defines a company as a living entity for its ability to learn and adapt and for its people to learn and grow.

All living systems must learn so they can adapt to changing environments or they will die. People also learn to adapt and they grow and expand from their learning. It is in the very process of putting forth their efforts to accomplish specific goals and desired results that creates the opportunity for learning. As people learn, they increase their capacity to contribute more energy.

Whether for a company or an individual, we can define the learning process as try something, determine the outcome, compare the outcome to the desired outcome and then determine what needs to be adjusted.

If this sounds similar to the process where we defined desired outcomes, assessed where we are today, determined the gap and then define initiatives to close the gap - it is. The process of determining a strategy and the process of learning are identical. All of life can be seen as a process of learning. Learning can also be viewed as expanding our capacity and capabilities to accomplish our goals. If you recall The Living Organization® model, there is the "contribution – learning loop."

The learning process starts first with having a goal and not being able to accomplish it. Does that sound odd – have a goal that you cannot accomplish? Well if you could accomplish it then you would have nothing to learn, would you? Learning requires having a desired outcome that you do not yet know how to accomplish. You try the actions you think will best achieve your desired outcome and compare the results of those actions to your desired outcome. The likelihood of getting it right is low at first. However, the process gives you new information you can use to adjust your actions. You repeat. After a while you will achieve what you set out to achieve.

Does this sound simple? Good, because it is except for the fact that most people are not willing to approach the achievement of the desired outcome from this perspective. They believe they must know how to accomplish the goal before they will set a goal. They have been caught up in the tyranny of expertise. We do not encourage learning because we expect people to already know.

In a conversation with one of our client companies, the founder voiced concern over some of the actions of the new CEO. The founder had groomed this younger individual to replace him. He fully believed he was the right person to take over the firm and that the new CEO had all the necessary skills. That is until one day the new CEO made a choice different than the founder would have made. The founder saw the error of this decision and was upset that the new CEO could not. I asked the founder how old he was.

"I am 72."

"And how long have you been CEO," I asked.

"40 years."

"And the new CEO, how old is he and how long has he been CEO?" "54 and in the position 1 year," he answered.

"And how smart were you when you started out and when you were 54?" I asked him.

"Oh, I guess he has to go through his own learning curve, doesn't he?"

In our drive to achieve results, we do not tolerate the learning process, but that is exactly what is required for continual improvement and continued growth. Growth by its very definition means I am more than I was. Growth is the expansion of my abilities through learning. One of Einstein's many quotes states that insanity is the desire to get different results while following the same process.

The Evaluate phase of the RTE-S™ process is the "contribution-learning loop" for the organization. It is the critical element for actual growth to occur. There are three specific areas that we recommend be included during the evaluate phase: performance against defined initiatives, behaviors against aspired core values, and key assumptions made.

How often should a company evaluate progress? Think of it in terms of the discipline of program management, a methodology for managing a large number of complex projects required to achieve an overall program objective. Strategy execution has a similar challenge.

Each initiative will be similar to a specific project in a program. Each initiative will have its own champion who will want to review progress against its goals. The overall strategy will also have to be managed to review the cross-initiative interactions, dependencies and timing. While every company is unique, we find that regular, quarterly reviews are the most effective. Just like a program has an identified individual, a Program Manager, responsible for the oversight of the total program, we suggest having an individual who is responsible for the oversight and coordination of strategy execution. Depending on how large and complex your organization is, you may choose to house that function internally or choose to outsource that function to a firm that specializes in execution management.

Who's leading the show?

In our model we specify a fifth key domain. In addition to People, Process, Customers, and Financial, we include the domain of Leadership. Leadership is more than just part of the people perspective. While leaders are first and foremost people, they carry an additional set of required skills in addition to the skills required of all people.

All people have the three skills identified in The ARC Framework® – functional skills, interpersonal skills and intrapersonal skills; and development of anyone requires the balanced development of all three skills. This is true for leaders as well. In addition, there are three requirements that are unique to leaders: management skills, team and collaboration building, and inspiration and motivational abilities.

Much research over the last couple of decades has focused on differentiating leadership from management. Unfortunately this is a false dichotomy. Every leader is a manger and every manager is a leader. Both require the same three skills. The only difference is that as you move up through an organization, the skills get applied in different proportions. A first line supervisor is likely to use more manage-the-process skills while a CEO will draw more frequently on the ability to inspire and motivate. This doesn't mean that a first line supervisor will not have to inspire and motivate nor does it mean the CEO won't have to manage elements of the process.

I believe our definition of leadership is outdated. If you look up leader in almost any dictionary you will get definitions like: the person in charge that guides and commands the troops. It is the man or woman at the top of the pyramid, the ultimate decision maker, the person who would say "the buck stops here."

Here is a different definition: a leader is a person who marshals resources towards accomplishing a desired outcome. These resources are people to contribute the energy, capital to enhance and leverage energy, organization to guide the flow of energy, and the vision of the future: all the elements required to manifest a desired outcome. We define a leader as a master of manifestation.

One last fallacy is that leaders are born, not made. Having worked with dozens of CEOs and many more leaders at all levels, I can tell you that no leader is born a leader. The best leaders are the ones who have learned along the way, usually from their failures. I shared my own story of my first year in management, and it has been my experience that every great leader has similar stories. The worst part of this fallacy is that the higher up the organization one goes the less likely they are to be offered any development support.

When I was at Hewlett Packard, it was an organization known for holding managers responsible for the development of their people. Yet this organization that pioneered many leadership development programs and tools ignored the development of its executive teams. When I was promoted to the executive ranks, I remember wondering why I hadn't gotten my regular performance review. One of my mentors and my closest friend, who had been promoted to Region Service Manager 18 months before me, enlightened me. "Management development, the HP-Way and MBO is for the regular folks. When you get to the executive level it is expected that you have already figured it out and you don't need development."

Later in life, I was talking with a fellow board member about the various individuals we might select for the CEO position. His comment was, "A CEO should already know how to do the job. If the individual needs development than he is not the right person for the job." I don't know about you but I don't know of anyone that cannot improve. What board of directors doesn't want their CEO growing in capability with the growth of the organization? Can the latter happen without the former?

Speaking of Boards

There has been much talk about boards of directors over the past decade. The rules of governance have been changing both by legislation and by serious self-reflection on the part of most boards. In the face of the scandals of the early part of this century, we saw the introduction of the Sarbanes-Oxley Act; and then as a result of the collapse of the financial markets, board governance again came under new regulatory requirements with the passage of the Dodd-Frank Act.

This has created a lot of conversations in governance circles, the academic community, and among directors. We have seen new guidelines come from the blue ribbon commissions of many governance organizations, from investor advisory services to the various exchanges and the SEC.

The last century has created an environment of compliance, where directors try to keep up with new rules and regulations that have emerged from these many agencies and work to ensure their governance practices are in line with best practices. What has been lost in all of this is the responsibility a board has to ensure that the company is growing and developing.

It is well accepted that a board has a fiduciary responsibility to its shareholders and I will not disagree. I will disagree with how this responsibility has been interpreted.

The responsibility is to grow the value of the firm and by doing that it will provide a return to those who invested in the firm. But what does it mean to create value? Following the energy model, it is the creation of goods and services perceived as valuable by customers and provided with the least consumption of energy. A board's role is to ensure the full development of the organization, starting with being proper custodians of its Soulful Purpose™, and to ensure that the organization is being true to its purpose and that its purpose is contributing to something greater than itself.

It must oversee the selection of the mission by which the organization will express its Soulful Purpose™. It must be vigilant that it is living by its core values. The board should also ensure that the Future Vision is stretching and challenging the organization to develop and grow so that is it can continue to meet the changing demands and needs of the communities of customers it serves.

The board should no longer rely solely on the CEO to ensure the company is executing. The board should be actively engaged to ensure that the journey to the future is also a journey of growth and development, for the company and for the CEO. To accomplish this, the board should embrace the discipline of a formal execution management process.

Viewed this way, the board will naturally align with the spirit of many of the regulations. Following the Strategic Compass™ will also create the following of a moral compass. One cannot honor one's Soulful Purpose™ without recognizing its meaning and contribution to something greater than oneself. One cannot be part of a community and not honor the relationships of that community.

One cannot fail to see the interdependence of all and will therefore make decisions that benefit all stakeholders. And it will be as silly to focus on the short-term gains as it would be to only consider the well being of your children for the next year. When we see the organization as a living being to nurture and develop, we will be concerned not just for this quarter or this year but for the long term.

The board, along with the CEO and the executive team, makes up the Leadership Team of the organization, the custodians of The Living Organization®.

If the CEO and the executive team are the parents, the board can be viewed as the grandparents, the wisdom council, the ones who can ensure and guide the growth and well being of The Living Organization®.

The Journey of Development

No one steps into a new set of skills simply by learning about it. It takes time and practice to go from awareness to integrated skills. There are well-defined stages of development. Think about any skill you have learned, whether it is a sport like skiing or golf, an activity like learning to ride a bike or driving a car, or intellectual skills like learning algebra or science. We always follow the same process. First is the awareness stage where we discover the value of developing the new skill and we commit to developing it. This is followed by the awkward phase where we are clumsy, uncomfortable, and ineffective as we struggle with the skill. Next we transition to the refinement phase where our practice is paying off, we have the basics down and we continue to improve the skill. This leads us to the Expert phase where doing the new skill is effortless and automatic.

The same is true for an organization's ability to improve its process skills. In fact there is a vast body of knowledge applying a developmental model to organization process skill development. This body of knowledge has been refined from the early days of the Quality movement with Phil Crosby's Quality Management Maturity Grid (QMMG) to the work of Carnegie Mellon University's Software Engineering Institute's (SEI) Capability Maturity Model (CMM®)[34].

To help companies better approach the process of creating an execution focused organization, we have developed the Execution Maturity Development Model™ (EMDM™). It defines five stages of development across a number of dimensions. The five stages are: Chaotic, Reactive, Structured, Proactive, and Integrative. The dimensions are The Arc Framework's® Leadership, People, Process, Customers combined with the four elements of the Strategic Compass™: Soulful Purpose™, Mission, Core Values and Future Vision.

Everything is a journey, a journey of development. The organization must develop as a collective to further its ability to meet the challenges of the future it desires to create. Leaders must develop their abilities to marshal the resources needed to manifest the desired results. The individuals within the organization must develop, learn, and grow, allowing for the full contribution of their unique gifts. And the board must provide the wisdom to ensure it grows in a healthy and robust fashion.

CHAPTER 13

"As human beings, our greatness lies not so much
in being able to remake the world - that is the
myth of the atomic age - as in being able to
remake ourselves." **Mohandas Gandhi**

The Journey Continues

For over 100 years, the business world has transformed our lives. The modern corporation has been the engine that has given us unprecedented prosperity. We have developed as a society more in the last 150 years than we have in the preceding 1,000 years. We have brought forth more innovation, created greater opportunities and improved the overall standard of living.

However, we now find the machine of production turning into a machine of destruction. Where it once served to advance our society, it now seems to be at the root of many of society's ills. From Enron to the recent collapse of our financial system, from environmental concerns to lack of societal responsibility, the modern corporation is becoming the center of evil in our world.

But the fault lies not in the inherent nature of the corporation but in the development, or lack thereof, of the true nature of business. Remember Edwin Lewis, Richard Geer's character in the movie *Pretty Woman*, who honed his business skills to win any deal no matter what it took. He soon discovered that though he won the battle for the deal, along the way he was losing the war for his soul.

Our businesses are living beings. They are not soulless machines that are only concerned with maximizing production and shareholder value. Yet that is what they have become. They have honed their ability to produce but lost their ability to contribute. But like Richard Geer's character, the story does not have to end here. There is another way.

Organizations are holistic, organic living beings. They are born to grow and develop to fulfill their Soulful Purpose™, a purpose that transcends the mere goal to produce goods and services, a purpose that calls for the organization to make a contribution to the market it serves and to the greater society.

The Living Organization® is not so much managed as it is guided and nurtured. The goal is to continually increase its capacity and its creativity. When an organization refocuses its attention to the realization and fulfillment of its Soulful Purpose™, it naturally transforms and begins to stand out from the crowd because of the magical results it produces. Companies like Whole Foods, Apple, and Trader Joes are but a few that demonstrate the magic of The Living Organization®. Examples such as Hewlett Packard, Wal-Mart and Toyota, who were once magical companies, show us that companies, like people, can also lose their way and like the Edwin Lewis character, find it again.

To help you understand the nature of The Living Organization®, we have shared the science behind the magic. We have explained how outcomes are the result of effective flow and transformation of energy. Even more significant, we revealed the nature of the three energy fields of Activity, Relationship and the all-important Context field.

The Context field is the source from which all energy emanates. It holds the key to intuitive insight and creativity. It is the ability to tap into and draw from this field that stimulates individual and organizational passion and engagement. The Context field is the source of all the magic.

The modern corporation has been on a long evolutionary journey from its birth in the mid 19th century as the culmination of the industrial revolution. The journey of the organization has been mirrored by the journey of those who have led them. At the beginning, the leaders focused on managing the organization to create an efficient machine. They found ways to streamline and optimize the workflow, creating metrics that provided the means to control the machine and the people who fueled it. Control and predictability were the key elements of success.

Around the middle of the 20th century, they recognized "people are our most important asset." The focus for the last 50 plus years was on teamwork and collaboration. We found ways to motivate and incentivize people to serve the machine better. Like assets, people were still components of the great machine of business. And like Anakin Skywalker of *Star Wars* fame, who chose to go over to the dark side and became the evil Darth Vader, business has firmly planted their feet on the path towards the soulless, money-first organization.

This soulless machine threatens to take over our world, even our humanity. But the journey does not have to end here. There is another way. There is the ability to breathe life back into our organizations, to restore its soul and the soul of all those who are part of bringing it to life.

Our leadership teams can learn to work with Context energy to discover and express the deeper purpose and meaning of their organizations. They can learn to create a culture and values that set the mold within the Context field that will guide the day-to-day behaviors and decisions of everyone toward the fulfillment of the Soulful Purpose™. They can learn the art of developing the whole person, supporting and enhancing the dignity of the human spirit, building a community of relationships that are bound together by a set of common ideals, communities of people who give to the community and in return receive from the community.

This is the new focus of organization leadership; set the context, develop the people, build communities and be in service. Coincidentally this is also the same role that has been at the heart of all spiritual leaders from time immemorial. One can extrapolate that the CEO will be the spiritual leaders of their communities in the 21st Century, a long way from how we have thought of the corporate CEO in the 20th Century.

This effort will lead naturally to organizations whose focus is more than winning and more than merely making money. We will create organizations whose focus is to be of service to its customers and society. Corporations that are Living Organizations® will naturally be socially responsible citizens that contribute to the welfare of their community, whether local or global.

This journey will not be easy. The power of the existing paradigm has a lot of energy behind it. It has been fueled by over 100 years of success. The financial community, which once served as a resource to support the good works of the corporation, has taken control and has bent the organization to its bidding. It will not easily relinquish this control and its demand for return on investment and quarterly profits that it sees as the core purpose of any business.

The challenges are neither onerous nor impossible. More and more leadership teams are stepping up and taking on these challenges. Though learning to work with the three fields of energy, especially the Context field, will at times feel awkward and perhaps even counter-intuitive, the rewards will outshine the efforts.

This is a noble challenge, one that goes to the root of what our corporations are (or should be). The modern business organization was once the great engine that drove the growth in our society. It still holds the promise of continuing its glorious contribution to the growth and wellbeing of our society.

We can discover how to work with the power of the Context field and nurture and enhance the organization's Soulful Purpose™. We can learn to weave the stories of creation and magically take us to a new world, a whole new dimension of what's possible. That's the Holy Grail that awaits anyone with the courage and conviction to find it.

Appendix

Business as the Driving Force of Society

For many years, society saw business as the great stimulator of progress, the engine that fueled the great advances in technology and living standards.

For instance, between 1760 and 1860, technological progress, education, and an increasing stock of capital transformed England into the workshop of the world. The Industrial Revolution set off a sustained increase in real income in England and later in the rest of the Western world[35] that has continued through to the present. With each passing year the rate has accelerated, giving the world standards of living far greater than anyone could have imagined just 100 years ago.

John V. C. Nye describes this progress in an article published in the *Library of Economics and Liberty*:

"Prior to the 17th century, most of the world not only took poverty for granted, but also assumed that little could be done about it. Even the most optimistic early writers could not imagine that more than a few percent of the population would ever be well off. Growth, if it could have been measured, was at most only a percent or two per decade.

"Yet the last few centuries have seen unprecedented growth. In the most successful countries, the average citizen now enjoys a material standard of living that would have made the greatest king of two hundred years ago turn green with envy…

"Even for the poorer areas, the so-called Third World, we find that per capita economic growth, improvements in life expectancy and declines in mortality from disease and malnutrition outstripped the performance of the most advanced nations of Europe, Britain, and France, during the Industrial Revolution of 1760–1860…

"What is unusual about the developed world since the 1700s is that… overall improvements in material prosperity seemed so modest that even contemporaries such as

Adam Smith did not appear to notice that they were living through what historians would later label the Industrial Revolution.

"Eventually, the changes were so dramatic that everyone could see that the daily lives of even the common laborers of Britain, France, Germany, and the United States had been greatly transformed.

***"The reason for this transformation was the accumulation of capital, which was due in turn to technological improvement and to the fact that these societies had large doses of economic freedom** [Emphasis added]. The twentieth century saw this transformation spread to a large part of the world."*[36]

Economic freedom allowed resources to move to where they could produce the most good. Economic freedom created opportunities for individuals to improve their conditions and advance their positions. Economic freedom was, and is, the foundation of our Capitalist System.

How Capitalism's Reputation Changed

Many now see this engine of growth that advanced society, once the cornerstone of economic development in the Western World, as the root cause of our current problems. People blame greed and the self-serving nature of Big Business for everything from the Great Recession to global warming to blatant disregard for the proper use of planetary resources.

True, Capitalism has always had its faults and its detractors. From Charles Dickens' Cokestown to William Blake's "satanic mills," authors have portrayed Capitalism as having a disturbing dark side that creates serious social problems such as child labor, unsafe working conditions, and abusive labor practices as a byproduct of progress. Government agencies responded to these problems with regulations like the minimum wage and child labor laws and the landmark Occupational Safety and Hazards Act of 1970.

As with all evolution, Capitalism took on many of the attributes of what came before. Though it replaced the old aristocratic society in which a small number of people controlled power and wealth and a large number of people had no power and little wealth, it exhibited many similar attributes. Yes, the aristocratic societies of kings and monarchs were overthrown and disappeared, only to be replaced by the owners and leaders of corporations and small businesses. The powerless many became their employees, were paid poorly, and again had little power over their lives. Many considered the corporations' employment practices oppressive.

This inequity created the reactive philosophies of Karl Marx and his followers, who believed that government had to exert centralized control as the only effective way to tame the dark-side of the free market economy.

In the struggle that followed, the Western World rejected this solution in favor of maximum individual freedom tempered only by certain regulatory controls. We still struggle to find the right mix of freedom and regulation, relying on a web of opposing forces, unions versus management, Democratic labor versus Republican Big Business, which seems never to agree on the proper balance.

The old model of Capitalism, while advancing society and creating great opportunities, favored the strong, the rich, and the powerful. But that has changed. Today, more and more, even the major beneficiaries of the Capitalist system, the corporations and their owners, are floundering or failing.

General Motors is a shadow of its former self, alive because the Federal government gave it billions of dollars. Other pillars of our financial system, such as Lehman Brothers and Bear Stearns, no longer exist. The days of the "imperial CEO" are ending and many individuals who invested their financial future in the Capitalist system lost 50% or more of their wealth when the financial markets crashed.

Countries such as Greece, Iceland and the once fast growing Ireland now face financial ruin. The United States, the most Capitalist of countries, is experiencing the greatest recession since the Great Depression because we continue to rely on decision-making models that are out of date and no longer effective.

Businesses are experiencing a constant onslaught of new technologies that change every aspect of the way we design, manufacture, sell and distribute products and services. The frequency of change is accelerating, adding further pressure to produce effective results and accelerating the rate of failure.

In the last ten years, we've had the dot-com crash, the fall of Enron, WorldCom, and Arthur Anderson, the collapse of the housing bubble, and the near collapse of our financial system. Once again, the government responds with governmental regulations ranging from Sarbanes-Oxley to the recent passage of the Dodd-Frank Reform Act, the greatest financial reform since the 1930s. This seems to paint Capitalism as the bad boy and has led to calls to reform the practices and foundation of business itself.

The Evolution of Business

The Industrial Revolution transformed the Western World. We transitioned from agricultural communities whose beliefs and activities revolved around the limiting cycles of nature to a society based upon logic and reason with rationally structured organizations. We went from dominantly individual contributions, the artisans, to collective organizations. This transition unleashed a tremendous amount of hidden energy that led to the rapid growth we have experienced over the last 100 years.

The original small organizations this transition produced evolved, requiring ever greater supplies of natural resources and capital to flourish. Eventually the first stock holding companies formed, bringing in a growing number of shareholders who gradually replaced the company founder and his family as the owners. Unlike the founders, who are personally involved and emotionally invested in the success of the enterprise, these new "owners" were distant from the company. Their only interest was to achieve a fair return on their investment. They left the management of the firm to a new group of players: the professional manager.

These new organizational leaders were not owners; they were agents of the owners whose jobs depended on the success of their enterprise. Therefore they needed models and techniques that would increase their chance of success. They knew that if they failed, the absentee owners would find someone who could succeed. The professional manager's search for efficient operations laid the foundation for our modern business principles and practices. It also paved the way for many of today's problems as well.

The Limitations of Worldviews

At any point in time, the range of solutions available to us is limited by our assumptions and worldviews. These become the lenses by which we see, interpret and understand the world around us. They help us survive and make sense out of our world. They also handicap us, for with their limited field of vision they invariably overlook important pieces of the puzzle.

We have all heard the phrase "perception is reality." The flip side is also true: "reality is defined by our perception." Worldviews are such an integral part of the environment we live in that they become part of us in ways we often don't understand. To fully understand our current worldview and the business model it created, we must understand the environment from which it sprang.

The world of the early 20th century was not, relatively speaking, very complex. Although conditions changed more rapidly than in the 19th century, we still didn't need sophisticated models to help us survive or adapt. In one generation, we might encounter three or four systemic changes such as the advent of flight, radio, and television that significantly altered the way we lived. We believed that we could, with a fair degree of confidence, predict the outcome of our decisions. Life appeared to follow a linear path of cause and effect that we as individuals and corporations could easily understand and follow. If we followed the right rules, our decisions would produce the outcomes we desired and we could predictably plan for the future.

The dominant scientific view of the day, laid down in the 17th century by the father of modern science, Sir Isaac Newton, supported this belief in predictability. In the Newtonian world, everything was linear, predictable and controllable. Newton perceived the universe as a machine that operated according to principles that could be dissected, explained and repeated. We found those truths to be self-evident and soothing so we integrated them into the design and operation of every one of our organizations.

The Organization as Machine

It logically followed, then, that when corporations appeared in the late 19th and early 20th centuries, they would form around the dominant scientific and mechanistic principles as those accepted by society. For instance, Frederick Taylor used the Newtonian assumption of an "orderly world" to create his now famous theory of Scientific Management. Like

Newton's universe, Taylor viewed business as a well-oiled machine whose only goal was to optimize the flow of activity to create maximum efficiency. Higher efficiency meant fewer wasted resources, which translated into higher production and profits. Precise, direct and simple.

Taylor's paradigm became the guiding principle for corporate organization and structure and is still used today. It viewed the organization as a simple cause-and-effect machine in which everything could be described, predicted, and controlled. In this model, leadership was based on the mastery of such mechanical skills as planning, organizing and controlling the activities of the enterprise.

In my early training as a manager it became clear that my role was all about leading the group I was responsible for. Leading meant taking the set of objectives given to us by those above me, who got the goals from those above them, and organizing my team to achieve those goals as efficiently as possible. I was the one who decided how the work would get done and who would do it. It was also my job to monitor and control the efforts of those that reported to me to make sure they were doing what the company expected. Workflow analysis, measures of output and efficiency studies to improve productivity were some of the tools I employed. While following this path provided some degree of success, I could sense these tools alone would not drive the level of performance I felt lay buried within my groups.

Until the middle of the 20th century, this control-oriented model served us well. It allowed us to tame nature and to transition from a dominantly agrarian society to a dominantly industrial society based on science and machines. It enabled the organization to use a predominantly low skill work force. It worked perfectly in an environment where change was slow enough that the world seemed orderly and predictable.

The incessant drive for efficiency ignored the various components of the machine. People were just another cog in the wheel of production that leaders plugged into the equation. Like other "machine parts," they were interchangeable. Leaders calculated cost by measuring how many men were needed to complete an assignment based upon the average number of widgets the average worker could produce.

We set our targeted revenue and worked backwards to determine the number of transactions it would take to achieve it. We added up the average transactions per employee, factored in a desired productivity goal, calculated the manpower required, and adjusted accordingly. This provided a straightforward, simple formula for success.

This simple, effective but impersonal paradigm began to break down in the middle of the 20th century as the environment evolved, revealing its shortcomings.

The Impact of World War II

As devastating as World War II was, it also had a positive impact on our society. Prior to the war, the country was still recovering from the Great Depression. The wartime economy achieved what all the New Deal programs could not: full employment. In 1940, 8 million Americans were out of work. After we entered the war, unemployment vanished. Even women joined the new production system, performing jobs once reserved for men. "Rosie the Riveter" became a popular American icon and image of progress[37]

The demands of wartime production required changes in factory operations that introduced new, more complex production techniques. Suddenly companies were no longer concerned with local markets. By 1943, half of all production went overseas,[38] requiring companies to acquire new skills and capabilities to address these new global markets.

When the war ended, the transformative changes continued. To avoid repeating the mistakes made after the First World War, when servicemen came home to find no jobs, few educational opportunities, and a housing crunch, Congress passed the Servicemen's Readjustment Act in 1944. The G. I. Bill (as it was popularly known) committed billions of federal dollars to support housing, education, health benefits, and job training for returning soldiers.[39]

In addition, unions asserted themselves with a wave of strikes that swept the nation. In 1946, for example, 400,000 miners struck not once, but twice. In all, 4.6 million workers struck at one time or another during that year. The power of the unions grew so strong that the Federal Government enacted the Taft-Hartley Act of 1947 to curb them[40]. This changed the face of the post-war workforce and the way managers managed it.

Our Changing Worldview

Not only did the war change our society, it also challenged our underlying worldview. The devastation wrought by the atomic bomb made the world aware of new scientific theories that revealed hidden forces that challenged the limiting theories of Newton's Classical Physics with its linear cause and effect relationships.

We entered the strange new world of Quantum Physics, which reframed our understanding of how the universe worked. The previous worldview of the "clockwork universe" fell to counter-intuitive concepts such as the Uncertainty Principle and Chaos Theory. The idea that the world was predictable and controllable lost ground.

For example, the Non-Locality principles of Quantum Physics stipulated that spatially separated systems could instantly influence each other no matter how far apart they were. A system on one end of the universe could affect one on the other side as if no time or distance separated them. How could fundamental barriers like time and distance no longer matter?

Another mind-bending theory of Quantum Physics was that quantum particles existed in more than one state at the same time. This concept, Superposition, claims that until we measure the state of the particle, it exists in all possible states simultaneously. The measurement itself limits the object to a single possibility. It reminds me of the question asked in my very first philosophy class, "If a tree falls in the woods and no one is there to hear it, how do we know it really fell?"

Changes from another field of science further altered our underlying assumptions. Psychology shifted away from the dominant Freudian view that followed the medical model of symptom, illness and cure. It no longer followed that symptoms could be traced back to a single causal illness, that psychology could be determined by the same cause and effect logic of Taylor's Scientific Management and the Newtonian worldview.

In contrast, the middle of the 20th century saw the emergence of Humanistic Psychology. Psychologists like Carl Rogers and Abraham Maslow cared less about what made us psychologically sick than what made us psychologically stronger. They felt that humans had an innate ability to move from a state of mere survival to a highly evolved, self-actualized state of being, a magical transformation that awaited all who worked hard enough to achieve it. This new view of human potential had a tremendous impact on how leaders would eventually view their employees.

Pushed by both the fields of physics and psychology, the business world rapidly underwent similar transformations. We witnessed changes in production methods, the nature of the workforce, and the birth of new corporate forms. The multi-national corporation emerged with its increased complexity and decreased predictability. Unions became as much a part of the power structure of the corporation as the once all-powerful CEO. And the workforce that returned from the war was different from the workforce that left.

Society changed. Internal organizational processes got harder to understand. A more complex world and changing workforce dynamics put enormous pressure on the old paradigm. As our business environment became more complex, the need to organize and control every aspect of operations pushed the new professional managers to their limits.

In the early days of the 20th century, we had a relatively unskilled work force and relatively simple production methods. It was relatively easy for managers to decide what to do and for workers to do what they were told. However, by the 1950's this was no longer the case. The increased complexity of production made it difficult, if not impossible, for a small group of executives to make all the decisions needed to address the many situations that could arise. In addition, the growth of multi-national corporations made it physically impractical for corporate executives to monitor every action of their far-flung enterprises.

Forces like these required that decisions be delegated to lower levels of the organization. Under this new system, mid-level managers and the workers they led suddenly had to make adjustments to work flow without any direction from above. This created flexibility and rapid responses to unanticipated situations, which was not possible in our old "top down" command and control structure. Employees had to be trusted to make the right decisions; they could no longer simply be cogs in a machine that did what they were told.

Many new jobs required a new level of sophistication and technical training that no longer made it feasible to swap out poorly performing labor units with better performing replacements. People were no longer interchangeable parts and individual performance could no longer be governed by a fixed set of rules and procedures that would automatically optimize returns and guarantee results. No longer a simple machine, our larger more sophisticated corporations took on a life of their own.

This forced the organization to focus even more on the role of their people and how they were developed and treated. They could no longer ignore the human factor. Treating people as interchangeable parts overlooked the unique set of gifts and talents each person possessed and it overlooked the obvious fact that not everyone worked or acted the same when plugged into the production process.

The Emergence of the Humanistic View

With the changes in worldviews and changing dynamics within the workforce, shouldn't the old rules for creating success in business change as well? Wouldn't the models for running companies change to keep up with the rapidly changing environment?

The sad reality was that much stayed the same. Even though unprecedented changes impacted their world order, management still clung to the Efficient-Machine approach of Frederick Taylor. They were still required to identify and eliminate blockages in workflow that created inefficiencies. They still had to determine the required amount of labor using established labor planning methods based upon the calculation of the average work per employee. The increasingly removed corporate level still used all of these "old school" methods and practices. Even with added complexity and changes in the environment, our corporate leaders continued to see their organizations as a machine they could master, providing them with a continued, but false, sense of comfort and control.

While viewing organizations as machines still worked on some level, it became clear that we needed a new model. If management wanted to get more out of their organizations, they would have to delve into the hidden world of the human psyche.

I was fortunate to develop my leadership skills in the computer industry during the 70s and 80s and especially at Hewlett Packard.

During this time the industry was entering its heyday of accelerated growth. To address the needs of this hyper growth many companies like Xerox, IBM, Digital Equipment Corp and Hewlett Packard adopted leading edge management principles to give them a competitive edge.

Management began to recognize that they could not fully explain the new challenges and forces by the simple, cause and effect paradigm of the "great machine of production." They could no longer ignore the human factor and the variations in performance it brought.

Therefore they explored what made people tick, what motivated their behaviors and what maximized the way they meshed together as a team. They had to identify and understand the forces that could decrease individual performance, disrupt team effectiveness, or create a blockage in the system, which led to a new focus on "people as our most important asset."

My management training programs embraced the teachings of humanistic psychology to better motivate employees and increase performance. Psychological theories such as Herzberg's Motivator-Hygiene theory, Maslow's Hierarchy of Needs and McGregor's Theory X / Theory Y became part of every manager's toolbox. I remember taking a class along with my peers and our boss, the Region Sales Manager, from Maxwell Maltz, author of *Psycho-Cybernetics*. In this class we learned techniques of self-hypnosis to reprogram our beliefs so that we could overcome our own limiting beliefs and hence perform at a higher level.

These new theories and frameworks served to re-orient how we viewed organizations and organizational leadership. Douglas McGregor's 1960 Theory X/Theory Y Management Styles model stated that two very different attitudes to workforce motivation existed. Theory X managers believed that employees were inherently lazy, disliked work, and would willingly avoid it if they could. They assumed that managers had to closely supervise employees and implement strict controls to ensure that people did what was expected.

In contrast, McGregor offered a new model: Theory Y managers who assumed that people were self-motivated, enjoyed work and could exercise self-control. I found this orientation to management to be consistent with my own experiences. The people who worked for me were not inherently lazy; they seemed to exhibit lazy behaviors as a result of the environment they were in. The so-called lazy behavior was a revolt against an environment that prevented them from doing what they loved. There was more to leading my team than just making them more efficient. I began embracing the new management theories of the humanistic psychologists.

I saw a lot of similarity between McGregor's works and those of Maslow. Theory Y was consistent with Maslow's view that people had a natural impulse to move up a Needs Hierarchy, shown in Figure 34 below, from basic survival to self-actualization.

Theories like these assumed that people naturally wanted to perform their best to reach their unrealized potential. If they did not perform well, it was not because they were lazy but because other factors got in the way. Accordingly, companies needed to provide the right environmental conditions and incentives under which employees could and would willingly work and succeed.

For McGregor, Maslow's needs could be grouped into lower order needs (Theory X) and higher order needs (Theory Y) and both could be used for motivation. Further studies also indicated that if an organization moved people up the hierarchy towards the higher order needs, performance would greatly increase.

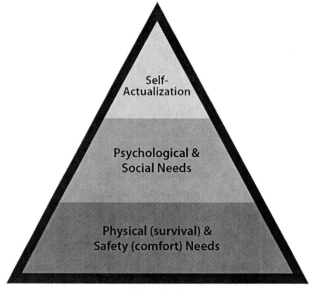

Figure 34

One such study was Frederick Herzberg's Motivation-Hygiene theory which argued that people were motivated by two different sets of factors: Motivating and Hygiene Factors. Motivating Factors would stimulate the desire to perform better, including achievement, recognition, responsibility, challenge, growth, and promotion. In contrast, Hygiene Factors only motivated when Motivating Factors were absent. Their absence could de-motivate but their presence did nothing to stimulate the desire to perform better. Hygiene Factors included pay and benefits, supervision, status, and working conditions.

Hygiene Factors correlated to Maslow's lower order needs and formed the basis for motivation by Theory X management styles, while Motivating Factors correlated with higher order needs and became the motivating focus for Theory Y managers.

This push for increased performance created a huge demand for books based on the theories of the new Humanist psychologists. Herzberg's 1968 article *One More Time, How Do You Motivate Employees?* had sold 1.2 million copies by 1987 and was the most requested article from the *Harvard Business Review*.[41] This demand for new approaches to management spawned the growing field of Organizational Development (OD) consultants who suddenly appeared to help develop methods for improving the worker's performance. Major companies allocated significant amounts of time and money to team building, employee development, pay-for-performance systems, motivation systems, and formal management training programs, all in the hope of better understanding and more effectively managing the key components at the heart of their machine's performance, those unpredictable parts we call people.

I began to incorporate many of these practices into my management repertoire. I took people through team building trainings where we would learn models of communication and that we all had certain behavioral and communication style preferences and that not everyone used the same styles. We practiced communicating with styles different from our own. Over the years I attended and even led many of these workshops. While they created great experiences and even some significant "aha" moments of insight and awareness, they didn't make a huge impact in the long run. We went to the offsite and returned on Monday morning to the same old patterns of behavior. So we would try another team building model, this time with different human behavior patterns. I have done the Disc instrument, Meyers Briggs, 16PF, Herrmann's Whole Brain model and countless others. And those are just for personality and behavioral styles. The same is true for the variety of sales models, interviewing models, performance management systems, change management, and all the rest.

One would think that with all of the evidence presented by the field of psychology, the evolving worldview offered by physicists, and the massive number of methods, processes and models provided by the OD folks this new focus on the "soft side of business" would change the foundational paradigm for good. But that didn't happen.

After years of proclaiming that, "Our people are our most important assets," companies still treated people as an instrument to be tuned instead of a person to be nurtured, developed and led. While hundreds of millions of dollars were spent on organizational development efforts and CEOs proclaimed the importance of people, training budgets were still cut first when times were hard. Although Herzberg developed his theory over 50 years ago and Maslow wrote his seminal work in 1943, Daniel Pink's latest best seller *Drive*[42] and Chip Conley's book *Peak*[43] still remind us that people are not motivated by money but by a sense of purpose and meaning

What happened? Why so little progress over the past 50 years? Why do managers still make critical decisions based solely on "that which can be measured?"

Like so many of my peers, I too found that something was missing. It was often hard to justify the expenses for such activities. I felt deeply that my people were the key to my success, but something else was happening, an almost invisible force that seemed to override all my efforts to truly empower my people. Yet at times I did manage to overcome this force as witnessed by the results I created.

In my job as Regional Administrative Manager for Hewlett Packard, I inherited what the company considered to be the worst performing administrative organization of the four U.S. sales regions. When I took over the helm of this listing ship in December 1982 the organization was just completing its five-star internal audit. This was an internal audit at the level of investigative depth that an external audit firm would perform. I was on the job no more the 45 days when we received the audit report. It consisted of a 39-page management letter. Being new to audit reports, my initial reaction when I read it was, "Great. They have done the deep dive and given me a wealth of information on areas to improve. The next morning, when I arrived in my office, Phil, the regional General Manager, came into my office and shared a personal note he had received from John Young, then CEO of HP. It said,

> *Phil, I read with interest your region's audit report and I am sure you will agree with me that we do not want to see this repeated.*
> *Respectfully,*
> *John*

Phil looked at me and said, "I do not ever want to receive another note from John like that!" He turned and left my office, leaving me with a clear understanding that I had inherited a nightmare. I soon learned that most management letters are less than a page long. Two pages meant you were not performing very well. This one contained 39 pages of concerns that I now had to deal with.

Within three years our regional administration team was considered the best performing organization not only in the U.S. but throughout the world. Admin managers from Australia, the Netherlands, France, England, and Germany visited us to see what we had accomplished. They all wanted to know what I had done that they were missing. We all used the same trainings, the same management tools and methods and yet somehow my results were far superior to the rest. Why? This is a question I couldn't answer myself. I would like to think I was just better at leading than they were, but I knew my peers and they were equally as talented in many ways, and in some ways I felt they were superior to me. I came to understand many years later that I had unconsciously broken through the barrier of the existing paradigm. I began to use a different model.

The highly acclaimed idea that "people are our most important asset" hints at why so many of my peers weren't able to accomplish the same results. Society and the dictionary generally define an asset as "as a valuable item to be owned." This is like thinking of employees as property, more like "slave labor" than "free-thinking, creative individuals." We may rationally recognize that people are not parts of a machine but we are still guided by language that emanates from a model created for a different time and different circumstances, a world that no longer exists. For some reason I was guided by a different model. I had broken the spell of the corporation as a machine and created results that to my peers and bosses looked like magic.

Humanism Isn't Enough

The Humanist phase of business evolution revealed the shortcomings of the dominant mythos, the mechanistic view of life. It altered our perception enough for us to realize that at the heart of every great company was a human component. It helped to explain some of the success of companies like HP when they lived the HP WAY or Toyota when they were committed to Total Quality with every part of their being. However, it also opened a Pandora's Box of unseen and seemingly uncontrollable forces that were still at work in our corporate organizations.

The Humanistic approach should have moved the business community away from the mechanistic model and brought us closer to a more organic vision of corporate structures and systems. That did not happen.

There are two explanations for this failure to change. The first is the enduring power of any existing paradigm. Newton's first law of motion reminds us of the power of momentum: *An object at rest stays at rest and an object in motion stays in motion with the same speed and in the same direction unless acted upon by an unbalanced force.* The forces that worked to maintain the existing paradigm overwhelmed any attempt to change it.

Adding to this natural momentum is the inability of the Humanistic perspective to fully explain all of the hidden forces that affect corporate performance and thus provide a way to work with those forces. People are unpredictable and inconsistent. While the Humanistic movement convinced us that people were critical to success, it did nothing to change the underlying paradigms.

The world is changing at an ever-increasing rate. What used to occur in 10 - 20 years cycles now occurs in 3 – 5 year cycles. The world moved from dominantly local and regional to increasingly national and international in reach. The simple gave way to the complex. What was long seen as predictable and controllable now appeared random and chaotic.

What happens when people feel out of control? For Maslow, they return to their lower order needs of survival and psychological well-being. They seek consistency, security and predictability, all the things promised by our old friend Scientific Management. The simplicity of the machine was too hard to give up, particularly when compared to the alternative complexity of a team of freethinking individuals. With a machine, everything could be measured, predicted and controlled. Not so with people.

Our original corporate system was designed to conform to our mechanistic view of the world. Business as a big machine was only concerned with production, which is measured by revenues and profits. This made making money the core purpose of our collective enterprise. The world of business became a race for financial returns, taking our once great engine of progress deep into a dark, hollow hole.

In 1981, Jack Welch, then CEO of GE, gave a speech at New York's Pierre Hotel, "Growing Fast in a Slow-Growth Economy." In it, Mr. Welch outlined his belief that companies must sell underperforming businesses and aggressively cut costs in order to deliver consistent increases in profit that would keep ahead of global economic growth. "GE," he told analysts, "will be the locomotive pulling the GNP, not the caboose following it." Though Mr. Welch says that he never said that maximizing shareholder value was the number one goal of the corporation, (he believed strongly that serving customers was the true focus of a corporation), this speech is often acknowledged as the dawn of the obsession with shareholder value.[44]

For whatever reason, the financial world, the business community, and society at large began chanting the mantra of "maximize shareholder value." This began the final transformation of Capitalism from a contributing force in society to its darker impulses. Business was now on its knees, bowing before the deity of the almighty dollar. Nothing else mattered.

Everything was measured by financial return. A new breed of engineer emerged: the financial engineer whose only purpose was the creation of financial wealth by whatever means possible. Using clever ways of reporting the numbers, they would often obfuscate the real performance of our corporations, making the results appear better than they truly were. They could package up a portfolio of assets and reapportion the risk across new types of securities, making an investment appear less risky and more valuable than it truly was. This is precisely what led to the financial meltdown of so many home based derivatives in 2009 and the near collapse of our entire financial system.

As a consultant I worked with a new CEO who was in his position for two years when he reached out to me for assistance. His predecessor was the founder of the company who at the age of 92 had passed away at his desk. This founder was admired for his passion for the products the company produced but was also considered a capricious tyrannical leader (the words of the employees, not mine).

The new CEO was committed to changing the culture and empowering his employees. He was a senior executive at one of the large beverage companies and had been through all the proper management training programs. He believed in Management by Objectives and setting a motivating goal that will stimulate outstanding performance. He committed to the board that he would grow the company from $50 million in revenues to over $100 million in five years. This became the single goal for his team and the organization. His attempts to implement a new culture and to empower the people were rooted in the underlying desire to improve the machine's ability to increase the production of profits. The result? He failed.

Like the company, our overall business community was no longer a machine driving progress but simply a printing press for money, a machine designed to produce more goods for more consumers in the endless race to expand market share and profits. It was wealth for wealth's sake. Our whole society fell under the spell of this hypnotic vision. Where business people once talked about improving people lives and putting a "chicken in every pot," money became an end in itself. This endless cycle of consumption and growth become the obsession of every professional manager and made us all slaves to the great money machine.

The Humanistic approach also fell prey to this addiction. If it couldn't be measured and reported, if it couldn't be directly related to growth in shareholder value, it had no merit. Managers were required to justify every decision in terms of return on investment, even the non-tangible benefits of developing people or building a culture of innovation. But as we now know, when everything is reduced to just dollars, it is difficult to invest in the intangible, unscientific creative processes that ultimately drive success.

Though the pull of the old always makes new ideas difficult to accept, it alone does not explain why the machine view was not more widely discarded. If the Humanistic approach truly held the value it professed, if it had been able to fully explain the world around us and produce the predictable results we still craved, then it would have overcome the resistance inherent in change. But history indicates that it neither failed nor succeeded. It shifted our focus away from an almost pure orientation to the machine and provided us with a greater understanding of the one part of our machine which we still couldn't fully understand, control or predict: people.

The Humanist model stressed the importance of people within organizations and increased the attention we paid to employee motivation and satisfaction. This paradigm evolved in tandem with science, which was moving away from the certainty of Newtonian physics to Quantum Physics and Chaos Theory. There was a growing recognition that organizations were more than linear machines or simple sets of processes and workflows. Instead, they were increasingly viewed as complex, non-linear, adaptive systems. Organizations were suddenly systems that could actually learn and grow.

For all its contributions, the Humanistic Model that emerged in the 1960's was never able to shift the underlying paradigm by which all decisions are made. We still believe in the dominant paradigm of the machine and its drive for measurable results even though we knew from the Humanist's theories that people were inherently difficult to measure or predict. We still do not know how to translate human benefits into machine metrics like return on investment to aid in making decisions.

The reason for the failure of the Humanistic paradigm to significantly shift our underlying paradigm was precisely because it could not and did not provide a substantive platform for new decision-making. It extolled certain benefits but couldn't explain them. It told us that unseen forces were at work but did not explore them. Without a deeper understanding of the underlying forces that produced the results, management had to take a leap of faith that things like "corporate culture," "human development" and "core values" created any real or tangible benefit to the bottom line.

At HP I knew my results came about because of the team I had. But there was something more than just the competence of the team. As a collective we operated at a higher level than the mere sum of the talents of the team. This team operated as if they were one unit. Even though they were geographically spread throughout the sales region, they were highly aligned and there seemed to be an energy that each member of the team drew from as if the collective added energy to each individual.

We know that when teams are "hitting on all cylinders" there is a sudden burst of energy we call Synergy, something almost everyone has experienced at one time or another. That is what I unconsciously created with my team at HP, a phenomenon in which the whole was greater than its parts, where $2 + 2$ suddenly equaled 5. Anyone interacting with my team could feel this heightened energy and could see it in the results we produced. But how do you explain it, much less harness its energy, for your own purposes? Can you create synergy with the same straightforward ease that you can realign the flow of work through the factory? We had the words to name it but not the understanding of how it worked that would enable us to create it. There are also many other areas that contribute to success that the Humanistic Model left unexplained.

How about harnessing creativity? Who would not want their employees to apply creative ideas to the challenges they faced? Yet with all the creativity programs out there and our desire for "outside the box thinking," we still have not succeeded in understanding how or why this magic takes place. Nor have we learned how to create cultures where creative out-of-the box thinking is the norm. Why?

Intuitive insights are also a key component in manifesting magical results. Where does this "sixth sense" come from and how can we tap into its power on a regular basis? It appears to be an ephemeral force that can't be counted upon to regularly produce results. Sometimes it works and other times it doesn't. When an executive's only justification for a certain decision is, "I have a gut feel about this one," are we more likely to listen to his instincts or reject them in favor of a more rational approach?

The Humanist paradigm failed to explain these common experiences and the power behind them. It failed to provide us with a formula to re-create these experiences at will. In short, it never explained the unseen forces at work that created the magical results that some companies like Apple, Southwest, Whole Foods and others regularly seem to attain. Nor can we explain why companies who have broken out of the pack and moved from good to great, fall from grace, companies like Enron, once considered the darling of Wall Street only to be the poster child for all that is wrong with business, and even my own beloved Hewlett-Packard, once considered the model of a company that had it right but which has been plagued with scandals of its own over the last decade.

Although we cannot explain or measure these magical forces, we know that some unseen power can have an incredible impact on the results we tangibly feel and measure. What if we could find a new model and a better understanding of these forces that is based on sound principles and does not require a complete leap of faith to put them into practice?

To find that "missing link" or the next stage in our evolutionary development, we've got to stop thinking of these hidden forces as mysteries and start thinking of them in scientific terms. We must learn to work with and release the latent energy that lies hidden and untapped within every organization, energy that, once released, will propel our corporations to new levels of achievement and performance. For that, we need a new way of understanding our world, a new paradigm that goes below our surface understanding to reveal the hidden forces at work in our world.

The Leadership Challenge

With each passing year and each passing crisis, today's new generation of leaders are experiencing the limitations of our existing business models and the devastating emptiness of many enterprises. They sense the need for something more, something drastically different. But few will change based solely on a leap of faith.

All change comes with uncertainty and a degree of risk. To embrace a new worldview, today's leaders need to know that the difficult changes being called for and the uneasy experience in venturing into the unknown will produce better results than they are experiencing today. They cannot be expected to make the changes based predominantly on the moral plea of "doing good in the world." Corporate Social Responsibility, Stakeholder Model, and other newly proposed models often set doing good above making a profit. At times it can even appear to oppose making profits, a message that invariably rings hollow to most corporate leaders and limits the adoption of these models. Organization leaders need a new model that better explains the world around them, one based on sound principles and science. One that provides them the necessary tools and empowers them to achieve better results than the model they currently use.

What would it take to create such a new model? Is there a scientific system that can explain the unseen forces of synergy and magical results to us in terms we can all understand and use? Such a model would ultimately have to explain the process of manifestation. It would reveal all the forces at work in our business and our world and how we can tap into and harness them to manifest the results we want to create. It could even show us how to spark our corporate creativity and breathe new life into our soulless machines.

Book References

When I look back on what has impacted and influenced me, bringing me to the perspectives I write about, there have been many experiences and many books that served as guides on my journey. My interest in how we, as humans, create brought me to explore many fields from physics to psychology, from science to spirituality and from management theories to Perennial Wisdoms.

There is no way I can include all of the material I think would be appropriate reading but I have included those pieces that have served to influence me the most and those I believe add to and enhance the conversation I started in this book.

Some of the books on this list may seem odd to some of you as reference for a book on business and organizations. For me practically everything on this list has served, in some form or fashion, to deepen my understanding of how organizations create results. They have merged and morphed so much with each other that is difficult to compartmentalize. Yet I have attempted to organize them so you as the reader can have a sense of the type of books they are.

There is one individual whose work I want to call out. It is the work of W. Brugh Joy. Brugh served as a very special guide for my personal journey over the last seven years. He opened gateways for me to explore and deepen my understanding into the Mystery of Life. Though he passed away in December of 2010, it is clear that his work lives on through me.

Browse the list and allow yourself to open to the books that call to you. Then go read them and see what new gates will open for you. Enjoy.

Changing the Business Paradigm

Firms Of Endearment by Raj Sisodia, David Wolfe, Jaq Sheth
The Living Organization by Lane Tracy
Be the Solution by Michael Strong and John Mackey
Managing in the Twenty-first Century by Satinder Dhima and Jerry Biberman
Let My People Go Surfing by Yves Chouinard
Origins of Wealth by Eric Beinhocker
Stakeholder Theory by Edward Freeman
Conscious Business by Fred Kofman
Liberating the Corporate Soul by Richard Barrett
SuperCorp by Rosabeth Moss Kanter
Wired to Care by Dev Patnail
Megatrends 2010 by Patricia Auburdene
Megatrend by John Naisbitt
Global Mind Change by Willis Harman
Future Shock by Alvin Toffler

Communicating

Everyone Communicates Few Connect by John Maxwell
Fierce Conversations by Susan Scott
Appreciative Inquiry by David L. Cooperrider and Diana Whitney
Getting to Yes by Roger Fischer and Scott Brown
Leading our Loud by Terry Pearce
The Leader's Guide to Storytelling by Stephen Denning

Deepening Our Understanding

The Living Organization: Spirituality in the Workplace by William A. Guillory Ph.D
Start with Why by Simon Sinek
Drive by Daniel Pink
Built to Last by Jim Collins
Good to Great by Jim Collins
Presence by Peter Senge, C. Otto Scharmer, Joseph Jaworski and Betty Sue Flowers
Fifth Discipline by Peter Senge

The Living Company by Arie De Geus

The Three Laws of Performance by Zaffron and Logan

Corporate Culture and Performance by John P. Kotter and James L. Heskett

The Seven Arts of Change by David Shaner

Working for Good by Jeff Klein

Strategy

Execution by Larry Cossidy, Ram Charan and Charles Burck

Balanced Scorecard by Robert S. Kaplan and David P. Norton

The Art of War by Sen Tzu and Ralph D. Sawyer

On Competition by Michael Porter

Blue Ocean Strategy by W. Chan Kim and Renee Mauborgne

Lords of Strategy by Walter Kiechel

Beyond Strategic Vision by Michael Cowley and Ellen Domb

Market Forces

Crossing the Chasm by Geoffrey A. Moore

Diffusion of Innovation by Everett M. Roger

The Innovators Dilemma by Clayton Christianson

The Experience Economy by Joseph Pine II and James Gilmore

It's Not what you Sell, It's what you Stand For by Roy Spence

Discovering the Soul of Service by Leonard L. Berry

The Myth of Excellence by Fred Crawford and Ryan Mathews

Tipping Point by Malcolm Gladwell

Leadership

Leading the Living Organization by Lane Tracey

Peak by Chip Conley

Tribal Leadership by David Logan, John King and Halee Fischer-Wright

Passion and Purpose by John Mackey

Leading with Soul by Lee G. Bolman and Terrence E. Deal

Edgewalkers by Judi Neal

The Servant by James C. Hunter

The Corporate Mystic by Gay Hendricks

7 Habits of Highly Effective People by Stephen Covey

The 8th Habit by Stephen Covey

One Minute Manager by Ken Blanchard

Now Discover Your Strengths by Marcus Buckingham and Donald O. Clifton

Leader Effectiveness Training by Dr. Thomas Gordon

As One by Michael Baghai and James Quigley

The Leadership Challenge by James M. Kouzes and Barry Z. Posner

Leadership in an Era of Economic Uncertainty by Ram Charan

Deeper Leadership

Appreciative Leadership by Diane Whitney

Getting Naked by Patrick Lencioni

The Mindful Leader by Michael Carroll

Leadership and the New Science by Margaret Wheatley

Inspirational Leadership by Lance H. K. Secretan

Conscious Leadership by Chutisa Bowman, and Steven Bowman

Unleashing Genius by Paul Walker

Authentic Leadership by Bill George

Mojo by Marshal Goldsmith

Are You Ready to Succeed by Srikumar Rao

Better Under Pressure by Justin Menkes

The Human Side of Enterprise by Douglas McGregor

Servant Leadership by Robert K. Greenleaf and Larry C/ Spears

Psychology

Man and His Symbols by Carl G. Jung

The Undiscovered Self by Carl G. Jung

The Portable Jung by Carl G. Jung, Joseph Campbell and R. F. C. Hull

Ego and Archetype by Edward Edinger

Anatomy of the Psyche by Edward Edinger

Creation of Consciousness by Edward Edinger

Positivity by Barbara Fredrickson

The Hero with a Thousand Faces by Joseph Campbell

The Power of Myth by Joseph Campbell

Emotional Intelligence by Daniel Goleman

Learned Optimism by Martin P. Seligman

Religion Values and Peak Experiences by Abraham Maslow

The Farther Reaches of Human Nature by Abraham Maslow

I'm Ok – You're OK by Thomas A. Harris

Psycho-Cybernetics by Maxwell Maltz

Flow by Mihaly Csikzentmihalyi

Please Understand Me by David Keirsey and Marilyn Bates

Lessons from Martial Arts

The Book of Five Rings by Maiyamoto Musashi and Thomas Cleary

The Art of Peace by Morihei Ueshiba, Lloyd James and John Stevens

A Life in Aikido by Kisshomaru Ueshiba and Moriteru Ueshiba

Man's Search for Meaning by Viktor Frankl

Spirituality in Business

Appreciative Intelligence by Tojo Thatchenkery and Carol Metzker

Spiritual Intelligence by Danah Zohar

The Workplace & Spirituality by Joan Marques, Satinder Dhiman, Richard King

God Goes to Work by Tom Zender

One by Lance H. K. Secretan

Purpose by Nikos Mourkogiannis

The Hungry Spirit by Charles Handy

Love and Profit by James Autry

Spiritual Fiction

Siddhartha by Hermann Hesse

Steppenwolf by Hermann Hesse and Basil Creighton

Demian by Hermann Hesse

Stanger in a Strange Land by Robert Heinlein

His Dark Materials Trilogy by Philip Murrya

Star Wars Trilogy by George Lucas

The Lord of the Rings Trilogy by J.R.R. Tolkien

Conversations with God by Neale Donald Walsch

Way of the Peaceful Warrior by Dan Millman

The Celestine Prophecy by James Redfield

Traditional Faith Paths

The Teachings of the Compassionate Buddha by E.A. Burtt

The Analects of Confucius by Arthur Waley

The Four Nobel Truths and other books by HH The Dalai Lama

Tao Te Ching by Lao Tzu

The Upanishads

The Bhagavad-Gita

The Torah

The New Testament

"Metaphysical" Physics

The Hidden Connection by Fritjof Capra

Dancing Wu Li Masters by Gary Zukav

Tao of Physics by Fritjof Capra

The Seat of the Soul by Gary Zukav

Personal Growth

Think and Grow Rich by Napoleon Hill

The Road Less Travelled by M. Scott Peck

The Different Drum by M. Scott Peck

The Happiness Advantage by Shawn Achor

The Purpose Driven Life by Rick Warren

Illuminata by Marianne Williamson

You Can Heal Your Life by Louise Hay

Invisible Acts of Power by Caroline Myss

Be Here Now by Ram Dass

The Power of Now by Eckhart Tolle

Living in the Light by Shakti Gawain

Awakening to the Spirit World by Sandra Ingerman and Hank Wesselman

Illumination by Alberto Villoldo

Fire in the Belly by Sam Keen

Knights Without Armor by Aaron R. Kipnis

Joy's Way by W. Brugh Joy

Avalanche by W. Brugh Joy

Endnotes

Chapter 1

1 "Appeal of iPad 2 Is a Matter of Emotions," By David Pogue, New York Times, Published: March 9, 2011
2 Arthur C. Clarke, "Profiles of The Future", 1961 (Clarke's third law)
3 See the appendix for a brief history of the evolution of business and the models that have supported its growth.
4 http://blogs.forrester.com/sarah_rotman_epps/10-07-22-apple_ipad_sales_why_tablets_are_even_bigger_we_thought
5 http://en.wikipedia.org/wiki/Force_field_analysis and http://en.wikipedia.org/wiki/Kurt_Lewin
6 Adam Smith, *The Wealth of Nations*, Book IV, chapter II, paragraph IX

Chapter 2

7 http://en.wikipedia.org/wiki/Invisible_hand
8 For more information about CSR visit www.csrwire.com. For Stakeholder vs. Shareholder visit http://www.valuebasedmanagement.net/faq_shareholder_stakeholder_perspective.html and for Conscious Leadership and the broader movement of Conscious Capitalism visit http://www.cc-institute.com/cci/
9 http://online.wsj.com/article_email/SB1000142405274870333800457523011266 4504890-lMyQjAxMTAwMDIwMzEyNDMyWj.html

Chapter 3

10 Feynman, Richard (1964). *The Feynman Lectures on Physics; Volume 1*. U.S.A: Addison Wesley.
11 For more details see http://wiki.answers.com/Q/How_many_thoughts_do_people_have_each_day#ixzz1IgbkE9KT
12 Bruce H. Lipton, "The Biology of Belief," pg 9, Published by Hay House, 2008

Chapter 5
13 http://en.wikipedia.org/wiki/Thermoeconomics
14 *"Welch condemns share price focus"*, Financial Times, March 12, 2009

Chapter 6
15 "Emotional Intelligence: Why It Can Matter More Than IQ," Daniel Goleman, Bantam Books, October 1995
16 Bruce H. Lipton, "The Biology of Belief," pg 9, Published by Hay House, 2008
17 Bruce H. Lipton, "The Biology of Belief," pg 9, Published by Hay House, 2008

Chapter 9
18 Michael Gershon, author of the 1998 book *The Second Brain* (HarperCollins).
19 Scientific America, February 12, 2010
http://www.scientificamerican.com/article.cfm?id=gut-second-brain
20 Institute of HeartMath® http://www.heartmath.org/research/science-of-the-heart.html
21 Neurocardiology, edited by Dr. Armour and Dr. Jeffrey Ardell
22 "The Blind Spot of Economic Thought: Seven Acupuncture Points for Shifting Capitalism 2.0 to 3.0, Otto Scharmer, Paper Prepared for presentation at the Roundtable on Transforming Capitalism to Create a Regenerative Society, MIT, June 8-9, 2009
23 Danah Zohar and Ian Marshall, *SQ: Ultimate intelligence* and Cindy Wigglesworth's, "Spiritual intelligence Assessment"
24 http://en.wikipedia.org/wiki/Spiritual_intelligence
25 For more information on this assessment tool visit http://deepchange.com/discover_skills/index
26 For more information on these movements visit: http://en.wikipedia.org/wiki/Corporate_social_responsibility for Corporate Social Responsibility, http://www.consciouscapitalism.org/ for Conscious Capitalism and http://hbr.org/2011/01/the-big-idea-creating-shared-value/ar/1 for an article By Michael Porter on the concept of Shared Value

Chapter 11
27 Excerpted from a Webinar by David Norton and Robert Kaplan, "An introduction to Execution Premium Process," © Palladium Group 2010.
28 Improving Organization Decision-Making through Pervasive Business Intelligence, 2009)
29 BSCol Research of 243 performance management professionals drawn from BSCol Online Community, march 2006)

30 ISO 8402, 1994

31 Rappaport, Creating Shareholder Value," 1986

32This quote came from The Balanced Scorecard Master-Class™, given by David Norton and Palladium group, October 2010. I modified it from their use as a definition for Balanced Scorecard to be more inclusive of performance management systems in general. While I believe theirs to be the most advanced there are others. Hoshin Planning is but one example.

Chapter 12

33 For a more detailed description of Business Model refer to Harvard Business Review Article "Reinventing Your Business Model," by Mark W. Johnson, Clayton M. Christensen, and Henning Kagermann, Reprint R0812C

34 http://en.wikipedia.org/wiki/Capability_Maturity_Model

Appendix

35 http://www.econlib.org/library/Enc/IndustrialRevolutionandtheStandardof Living.html

36 http://www.econlib.org/library/Enc/StandardsofLivingandModernEconomi cGrowth.html

37 http://us.history.wisc.edu/hist102/lectures/lecture21.html

38 http://wiki.answers.com/Q/How_did_World_War_2_affect_the_US_econom y

39 http://en.wikipedia.org/wiki/G.I._Bill

40 http://us.history.wisc.edu/hist102/lectures/lecture22.html

41 Herzberg, F.I. 1987, 'One more time: How do you motivate employees?' *Harvard Business Review*, Sep/Oct87, Vol. 65 Issue 5, p109-120 (*note: the reference to sales numbers is in the abstract written by the editors.*)

42 "Drive: The Surprising Truth About What Motivates Us," Daniel H. Pink, Riverhead Hardcover, December 2009

43 "Peak: How Great Companies Get Their Mojo from Maslow," Chip Conley, Jossey-Bass, September 2007

44 http://en.wikipedia.org/wiki/Shareholder_value - and also - http://www.ft.com/cms/s/0/294ff1f2-0f27-11de-ba10-0000779fd2ac.html?nclick_check=1

Index

7-Eleven, 92

Activity Field, 2, 3, viii, 7, 22, 28, 41, 43, 56, 75, 76, 77, 78, 80, 81, 82, 83, 86, 87, 88, 91, 93, 97, 98, 99, 103, 104, 108, 109, 110, 112, 113, 114, 115, 116, 117, 118, 119, 120, 121, 122, 123, 124, 125, 126, 129, 133, 136, 137, 138, 139, 143, 148, 152, 157, 158, 159, 160, 162, 164, 166, 169, 170, 171, 183, 186, 194, 197, 207

Adelphia, 69

Alignment, ix, 22, 54, 79, 111, 148, 149, 152, 153, 158, 159, 160

Amazon, 15

Apple, 13, 14, 15, 16, 18, 19, 23, 29, 84, 93, 121, 140, 186, 215
iPad, 13, 18, 233
iPhone, 13, 18

Arc Framework, 136, 184

Armour, Dr. J. Andrew, 108

Arthur Anderson, 194

Balanced Scorecard, 133, 134, 136, 137, 172, 221

Bear Stearns, 13, 69, 194

Bernanke, Ben, 22

Blake, William, 192

Blue Ocean Strategy, 132, 133, 221

BMW, 15

Boeing, 145

Boesky, Ivan, 71

Capability Maturity Model, 184

Capitalism, vii, ix, 9, 12, 17, 18, 19, 20, 23, 67, 111, 192, 193, 194, 211, 233

CarMax, 15

Caterpillar, 15

Chaos Theory, 199, 213

Clark, Arthur C., 15, 233

Coca-Cola, 110

Collins, Jim, 29, 220

Commerce Bank, 15

Commitment Alignment, 160

Container Store, 15, 23

Context Field, 1, 2, 3, v, viii, 75, 97, 98, 99, 101, 104, 106, 107, 108, 109, 110, 112, 113, 114, 115, 116, 117, 118, 120, 121, 122, 123, 124, 127, 128, 129, 130, 133, 136, 138, 143, 145, 148, 151, 152, 153, 155, 158, 160, 162, 165, 166, 169, 171, 186, 187, 188, 189

Core Values, ix, 10, 143, 144, 148, 149, 153, 178, 182, 184, 214

Corporate Social Responsibility, 30, 31, 111, 216

Corporation, 1, 9, 17, 26, 30, 32, 50, 59, 60, 70, 71, 72, 120, 123, 130, 148, 175, 185, 187, 188, 201, 209, 211

Costco, 15

Creation, i, iii, vii, 16, 18, 19, 33, 36, 42, 45, 48, 55, 69, 87, 121, 122, 137, 146, 165, 173, 182, 189, 211, 223

Crosby, Phil, 184

Cultural Alignment, 160

Customers, 1, 4, 7, 8, 10, 11, 12, 15, 30, 33, 34, 43, 54, 56, 58, 59, 65, 70, 72, 73, 79, 92, 93, 94, 95, 100, 104, 122, 123, 124, 126, 127, 129, 130, 133, 136, 139, 143, 145, 146, 147, 164, 166, 167, 176, 179, 182, 184, 188, 211

de Geus, Arie, 176
Delphi Analysis, 132
Deming Cycle, 135
Dickens, Charles, 192
Disc, 206
Dodd-Frank Act, 181
eBay, 15
Economic Freedom, 192
Edwards Lifesciences, 145
Einstein, Albert, 17, 25, 35, 36, 38, 41, 178
Emotional Intelligence, 80, 110, 164, 223
Enron, 69, 71, 185, 194, 215
Environmental Scanning, 132
Epps, Sarah Rotman, 18
Esalen, 1, 33
Evolution, 2, iv, vii, ix, 8, 10, 16, 24, 36, 49, 50, 65, 102, 104, 187, 193, 194, 209, 216, 233
Execution Management, 133, 135, 136, 155, 179, 183
Execution Maturity Development Model, 184
Execution Scorecard, 164
Experience, 1, 2, vi, viii, 7, 23, 29, 35, 39, 40, 42, 45, 46, 49, 56, 78, 79, 84, 85, 87, 91, 92, 93, 94, 95, 97, 104, 106, 107, 109, 111, 112, 132, 138, 147, 153, 155, 170, 180, 216, 221
Federal Reserve Bank, 22
Feynman, Richard, 38
Financial, 2, 7, 22, 63, 64, 67, 69, 70, 122, 123, 124, 136, 179, 181, 185, 188, 194, 211, 233
Fiorina, Carly, 68

Firms of Endearment, 14, 31, 121
Five Force Analysis, 132
Force Field analysis, 19
Future Vision, v, vi, ix, 29, 71, 72, 73, 111, 143, 144, 147, 153, 157, 173, 180, 182, 184, 195, 210, 212, 221
General Electric Corporation, 70
General Motors, 13, 18, 29, 194
Gershon, Michael, 107
Goal Alignment, 159
Goldman Sachs, 69
Goleman, Daniel, 80, 110, 223
Google, 15
Great Depression, 194, 198
Great Recession, 192
Gretsky, Wayne, 88
Harley-Davidson, 15
Harvard Policy Model, 134
Heart-brain, 108, 109
HeartMath Institute, 108
Herzberg, Frederick, 203, 205, 206, 207
Hewlett Packard, 3, 4, 25, 29, 37, 43, 67, 68, 72, 100, 101, 110, 181, 186, 203, 207, 209, 214
Honda, 15
Hoshin Planning, 135
Human Capital, 136
Humanism, x, 200, 202, 203, 204, 206, 209, 210, 213, 214, 215
Hurd, Mark, 68
IBM, 29, 203
IDEO, 15
IKEA, 15
Improv, 175, 176
Industrial Revolution, 18, 187, 191, 192, 194
Information Capital, 136
Innovation Strategy, 167, 169
Invisible hand, 22, 29, 111
JetBlue, 15
Jobs, Steve, 14, 29

Johnson & Johnson, 15
Jung, Carl, 23
Kaplan, Robert, 132, 136, 155, 221
Keating, Charles, 71
Knowledge Systems, 81
Leadership, 3, iv, x, 5, 6, 26, 30, 47, 111, 122, 123, 124, 125, 134, 147, 149, 179, 180, 181, 183, 184, 187, 188, 197, 203, 204, 216, 222, 223, 233
Lehman Brothers, 13, 18, 69, 194
Lewin, Kurt, 19
Living Customers, 94
Living Entities, 94
Living Organization, 1, 2, 3, 4, i, ii, iii, vi, vii, 5, 6, 7, 10, 11, 25, 26, 27, 29, 33, 34, 36, 51, 52, 53, 54, 55, 58, 60, 67, 86, 88, 90, 94, 101, 112, 120, 121, 123, 124, 128, 136, 137, 142, 147, 155, 159, 177, 183, 186, 188, 220, 222, 224
Lord Kelvin, 38
Machine, 1, ix, 6, 7, 9, 10, 14, 18, 26, 28, 29, 30, 31, 32, 77, 93, 110, 111, 119, 120, 122, 123, 147, 185, 187, 196, 197, 198, 201, 202, 203, 206, 209, 210, 211, 212, 213, 214
Madoff, Bernard, 69, 71
Magic, 2, vii, viii, 1, 6, 14, 15, 16, 17, 19, 21, 23, 25, 26, 27, 28, 29, 34, 37, 60, 84, 85, 95, 97, 111, 122, 147, 149, 175, 176, 186, 187, 200, 209, 215, 216, 217
Maltz, Maxwell, 203, 223
Management, 4, 3, 4, 7, 8, 11, 25, 26, 34, 42, 84, 99, 111, 119, 122, 123, 125, 133, 134, 135, 137, 162, 168, 172, 179, 180, 193, 195, 202, 203, 204, 206, 208, 212, 214, 219

Maslow, 1, 129, 200, 203, 204, 205, 206, 207, 210, 223
Mauborgne, Renee, 132, 221
Maxwell, James Clerk, 21, 22, 29, 203, 221, 223
Mayer, Emery, 108
McDonalds, 92
McGinnis, Bill, v, 17
McGregor, Douglas, 203, 204, 205, 223
McKinsey, 110
Merck Pharmaceuticals, 110
Meyers Briggs, 206
Microsoft, 22
Milken, Michael, 71
Mission, ix, 5, 53, 54, 86, 93, 111, 143, 144, 145, 146, 153, 182, 184
National Technical Systems, v, 17
New Balance, 15
New Deal, 198
New York Times, 3, 22, 233
Newton, Isaac, 38, 136, 196, 197, 199, 210
Physics, 29, 34, 213
Nokia, 110
Nordstrom, 93
Norton, David, 132, 136, 155, 221
Nye, John V. C., 191
Organization Capital, 136
Patagonia, 2, 15
Peets, 92
Performance Management, 137
Planning Horizon, 139, 140, 141
Pratt & Whitney, 2, 4, 100
Process Reengineering, 59, 126
Profit, vii, viii, 12, 30, 31, 60, 63, 64, 65, 66, 67, 68, 69, 70, 71, 72, 211, 216, 224
Quality Management Maturity Grid, 184
Quality Movement, 135

Quantum Leaders, ii, vi, 5, 72, 73, 110
Quantum Physics, 21, 112, 199, 200, 213
Rankin, William, 38
Real Time Execution System, ii, ix, 7, 136, 155, 157, 161, 162, 163, 172, 178
  align, 155, 156
  assess, 155, 158, 159, 161, 164
  decide, 155, 158, 159, 161, 172
  define, 155
  evaluate, 155, 158, 159, 164, 174, 178
  perform, 155, 158, 159
Reductionist, 34, 35
REI, 15
Relationship Field, 2, 4, v, viii, 2, 10, 33, 35, 40, 45, 49, 62, 67, 75, 77, 78, 79, 80, 81, 82, 83, 86, 87, 88, 89, 90, 91, 93, 94, 95, 97, 98, 104, 105, 108, 109, 110, 112, 114, 118, 120, 122, 123, 124, 126, 127, 129, 133, 136, 138, 148, 158, 160, 162, 164, 165, 166, 169, 171, 186
Sarbanes-Oxley, 181, 194
Scenario Planning, 132
Scharmer, Dr. Otto, 109, 220
Scientific Management, 34, 197, 200, 210
Scientific Method, 34
Senge, Peter, 176, 220
Shared Value, 111
Shareholder Value, 14, 33, 70, 71, 138, 186, 211, 213
Shell, 110, 176
Sisodia, Raj, 14, 220
Six Sigma, 59, 126
Smith, Adam, 9, 21, 29, 192, 233
Social Psychology, 19
Soulful Purpose, 2, ii, v, viii, 53, 54, 67, 68, 101, 102, 103, 118,

119, 122, 129, 130, 143, 144, 145, 146, 147, 151, 153, 157, 174, 176, 182, 183, 184, 186, 187, 189
Southwest, 15, 215
Spiritual Intelligence, 1, 110, 165, 224
Starbucks, 15, 92, 93, 95, 110
Strategic Compass, ii, 143, 153, 155, 157, 158, 159, 160, 163, 183, 184
Strategic Planning, viii, 20, 134, 135, 139, 142, 152, 171
Strategy, viii, 70, 72, 111, 122, 131, 132, 133, 134, 135, 137, 139, 140, 155, 160, 161, 164, 167, 168, 169, 170, 172, 173, 174, 177, 179, 221
Strategy Execution, viii, 132, 134, 139, 155, 164, 168, 169, 179
Sun Tzu, 134
Synergy, viii, 7, 28, 81, 83, 84, 85, 95, 214, 217
Taylor, Frederick, 119, 197, 202
Thales of Miletus, 38
Timberland, 15
Total Quality Management, 59, 126
Toyota, 15, 186, 209
Trader Joe's, 15, 93
Tyco, 71
Uncertainty Principle, 199
Unilever, 110
UPS, 15
Wall Street Journal, 31
War Gaming, 132
Watts, Alan, 2
Wegmans, 15
Welch, Jack, 53, 70, 211, 233
Whole Foods Market, 9, 10, 15, 23, 84, 93, 121, 186, 215
Wigglesworth, Cindy, 1, 165
Young, Thomas, 38

About the Author

Throughout his professional career as a Chief Executive Officer, Corporate Director, and Advisor to CEOs, Norman Wolfe has successfully guided corporations through major transitions leading to substantial growth, market expansion and enhanced financial performance. Currently, he is the Chairman and CEO of Quantum Leaders, a leading edge consulting company guiding boards and CEOs to improve strategy execution.

Norman's lifelong passion has been to understand how we, as individuals and organizations, create results and manifest our destiny. This passion is brought to life through his own Soulful Purpose™ to transform organizations to support and enhance the dignity of the human spirit in the process of serving their community. The Living Organization® Trilogy is the part of that journey.

Norman travels the country speaking and training organizations and leaders on The Living Organization® and the way to transform organizations from machines of production to dynamic, creative living organizations. His company, Quantum Leaders Consulting provides tools, assessments, training and implementation support to companies wanting to become Living Organizations®. To have Norman speak at your next event, please visit his website www.normanwolfe.com. For training, consulting or implementation support, visit www.quantumleaders.com.

Norman currently resides in Irvine, CA with his wife Jane and their two Bichon dogs. He is also an Ordained Interfaith Minister offering spiritual guidance and insightful dialogue. He welcomes feedback and conversation and can be reached at nwolfe@quantumleaders.com.

CPSIA information can be obtained at www.ICGtesting.com
Printed in the USA
BVOW051351190911

271493BV00004B/5/P

9 780983 531012